Economic Education

Economic Education

INVESTING IN THE FUTURE

by
G. L. Bach
W. Lee Hansen
Marilyn Kourilsky
Mary Ellen Oliverio
Walter E. Williams

*Introduced and
Edited by*
William H. Peterson

The
Burkett Miller
Memorial Lectures
on Economic Education

The University of Tennessee Press / Knoxville

Publication of this book has been aided by a grant from the Center for Economic Education, The University of Tennessee at Chattanooga.

COPYRIGHT © 1982 BY THE UNIVERSITY OF TENNESSEE PRESS / KNOXVILLE.
ALL RIGHTS RESERVED.
MANUFACTURED IN THE UNITED STATES OF AMERICA.
FIRST EDITION.

Clothbound editions of University of Tennessee Press books are printed on paper designed for an effective life of at least 300 years, and binding materials are chosen for strength and durability.

Library of Congress Cataloging in Publication Data

Main entry under title:
Economic education.
   Bibliography : p.
   Includes index.
   1. Economics—Study and teaching—United States—Addresses, essays, lectures. I. Bach, George Leland, 1915–   . II. Peterson, William H.
HB74.8.E25   330'.07'073   81–11449
ISBN 0–87049–333–7   AACR2
ISBN 0–87049–334–5 (pbk.)

Contents

Introduction by William H. Peterson   1

I: Economic Education and America's Love-Hate Affair with Business by G. L. Bach   11

II: Are Americans Economically Literate? An Appraisal by W. Lee Hansen   22

III: Experience-Based Learning by Marilyn Kourilsky   38

IV: Who Is Responsible for Economic Education—Parents, Teachers or the Public School System? by Mary Ellen Oliverio   54

V: Economic Education and Minorities by Walter E. Williams   74

Biographical Information   88

Index   93

Introduction
by William H. Peterson

Is economic education important to the future of America?

Consider this. According to the Joint Council on Economic Education, a recent survey of 15,000 junior high school students indicated that only 23 percent could correctly identify a simple description of the capitalistic system, and that only 50 percent could differentiate between the obvious characteristics of the U.S. and the U.S.S.R. economies.[1] And their elders don't appear that much smarter in the realm of economics. According to an opinion poll of the general public, 37 percent of the respondents could not relate any aspect of their personal lives to the profitability of American business.[2] And 24 percent responded that they "don't know" when asked to define "private enterprise."[3]

Responses of this sort apparently prompted the U.S. Senate to resolve: "A widespread understanding of the operations and problems of the United States economic system is essential if Americans are to meet their responsibilities as citizens, voters, and participants in a basically private enterprise economy."[4] Former AT&T Chairman Frederick R. Kappel was blunter still: "If we have enough voters totally ignorant of economic pros and cons, they can vote this country down the drain without even knowing it."[5]

---

[1] *Economic Illiteracy: Can We Afford It Any Longer?* New York: Joint Council on Economic Education, c. 1979, p. 5.
[2] *Idem.*
[3] *Idem.*
[4] U.S. Senate Resolution 316, 89th Congress.
[5] *Economic Iliteracy*, p. 2.

Such data and comments suggest that many, if not most Americans have never had any formal education in economics during their formative years. In any event, such was the general background of economic literacy in the fall of 1978 and spring of 1979, when the Center for Economic Education of the University of Tennessee at Chattanooga presented as its first public activity the Burkett Miller Memorial Lectures in Economic Education. Those lectures form the basis of this book.

The contributors to this inaugural series are all outstanding scholars and teachers; several of them have held impressive positions in government and business. The combined knowledge and experience of these men and women creates, I believe, a pool of innovative thought which can help advance the neglected field of economic education.

Economic education is an idea whose time has come. Rising economic pressures and conflicting explanations have combined to produce much public confusion about the nature and causes of unemployment, inflation, poverty, foreign competition, lagging or falling real personal income, and other important topics. In addition, the relative absence of a basic economic literacy among the American public has created an atmosphere in which realistic debate about economic policies becomes difficult at best.

To help correct this situation, especially through the medium of our elementary and secondary schools, is the aim of the five scholars whose Burkett Miller Lectures comprise this volume. Each scholar serves in a way to reinforce and augment the findings and conclusions of the others. All are convinced that economic education can enhance the quality of American life and help arrest if not cure the "arteriosclerosis" that seems to be spreading throughout the American economy.

In the first lecture Professor G. L. Bach of Stanford makes the point that economic educators must first face up to America's love-hate affair with big business; this ambivalence, among teachers as well as students, inhibits clear thinking on economic problems. Professor Bach says that if economic educators are to make any headway, they must be cognizant of this preconditioning problem.

He counsels both educators and businessmen. To educators he

says "economics is a way of thinking about problems; it provides us with analytical tools. The job of economic educators is to teach students to apply those tools to the economic problems we face. It is not propaganda, not cant." Facts, too, must be set straight, notes Dr. Bach. Profit on sales, for example, do not average 30 or 40 percent as most Americans believe, but more like 5 percent.

To businessmen Dr. Bach says they must earn the legitimacy they so earnestly crave. Scandals such as multinational corporations engaging in kickback schemes overseas serve to undermine the case for legitimacy and set back the cause of economic education. Also, the job of business, insofar as the public is concerned, is not to make profits but rather to *earn* them, to produce the goods and services that "the public wants at reasonable prices and [provide] steady jobs at reasonable pay." Dr. Bach reminds businessmen they have "no God-given right" to profits.

Professor W. Lee Hansen in his paper paints a wider canvas, depicting the dimensions of economic literacy—and illiteracy—and the steps being taken to broaden economic understanding, an understanding that he believes is crucial to the success of our democratic society. He concurs with Dr. Bach that much knowledge of economics is really "folk" knowledge and needs retooling in basic facts and theory. He notes surveys showing that what most people know about economics comes from their personal experience and that most people see their role in the economic system as a passive one. He says that, although several states have mandated some form of economics instruction, the pressure behind these mandates is not strong.

Economics is not a popular field of study, concedes Professor Hansen, and he holds the economics profession partially to blame for this. Economics "is often seen as dull, difficult and too mathematical." Students are often confused or fail to see any personal relevance in it.

Can the study of economic education be made more attractive? Maybe. *If* it can be made more dynamic and more relevant. Dr. Hansen notes that often economics is projected as either economics for "citizenship" or economics for "personal choice." Citizenship economics focuses mainly on alternative government policies, with negligible benefits to individuals. Personal choice or consumer economics is frequently "viewed as something else, not economics." Dr. Hansen believes one educational solution is to play up the usefulness of choices, of giving up one thing for another, "of the economic concept of 'trade-offs' [which] can be demonstrated at both the personal and societal levels—e.g., a new car or a college education at the personal level, guns or butter at the societal level."

Dr. Marilyn Kourilsky of UCLA's graduate school of education also believes economics instruction can be enhanced through better content, but she stresses *methodology*, especially for elementary and secondary school students. She submits that economics should not be taught by "talking at the children" for several hours a day when they are already exposed to an average of five hours a day of television at home. Instead she opts for experience-based instructional programs, for learning by doing, for having students make real economic choices and experience the outcomes. The learner thus becomes *part* of the action, and the lesson sticks, holds Professor Kourilsky.

Accordingly she offers the KEEP (Kourilsky Economic Education Programs) series—Kinder-Economy (grades K–2), Mini-Society (grades 3–6), and Max-Economy (junior and senior high). She says these programs, especially the Mini-Society program, have demonstrated increases in a young person's self-concept, assertiveness, autonomy, and positive attitude toward school and learning, as well as achievement in math and reading.

In the Mini-Society, Dr. Kourilsky explains, children create their own currency and then see how scarcity (limited resources versus relatively unlimited wants) is the central economic problem and impetus for any economy. They bid competitively for the limited resources—felt-tip pens, for example—and thus settle the question of who gets them. They make and sell goods and services, even developing banks and insurance companies. Some become salaried workers, others go into business for themselves. The teacher guides the activity and helps them learn the relevant economic principles involved.

Dr. Mary Ellen Oliverio is more concerned with content than with methodology and in her lecture raises the question: "Who is responsible for economic education—parents, teachers, or the public school system?" Her answer is that all are. The responsibility is shared, but the question for optimizing economic understanding is: How?

Within the public school system the sharing extends to the local school board, system superintendent, curriculum directors, and school principals. All these officials, says Dr. Oliverio, should see how their three-fold responsibility of transmitting our cultural heritage, developing critical thinking, and generating intellectual skills should in turn lead to the appropriate inclusion of economic understanding throughout the school program.

She notes further how teachers implement the goals of the school system, how they have to design and redesign what is to be provided in the way of learning in the classroom, and how they help young people grow up and live successfully in an industrial world.

For the junior and senior high school teachers of social sciences this means sensitively dealing with such knotty problems as technology, population, energy, inflation, urban renewal, foreign competition, and the "interdependency of nations." She recognizes the controversial nature of such problems and urges the teacher to help the student sift "fact from value, description from analysis, first approximation from detailed revelation."

Parents of course are responsible for encouraging their children's study, and providing broad economic and moral values. Dr. Oliverio sees such values as having a constructive impact on child behavior in particular and economic behavior in general.

In his lecture Professor Walter E. Williams is also concerned with content in economic education and he, too, raises a question for economic educators: "Are your means—i.e. program content—really in accord with your laudable end?" What he is questioning is the soundness of certain principles employed in economic education, especially when those principles are embodied in questions of public policy.

As a black economist, Dr. Williams focuses on policy that seeks to help minorities and inadvertently ends up hurting minorities. For example, he is critical of the minimum wage law and wonders how we "help less fortunate people by destroying their best alternatives." He argues that the law discriminates against those workers whose output is less than the legislated minimum. Such discrimination is especially hard on the young, he holds, pointing to the lamentable fact that black teenager unemployment ranges up to seven times the national average.

In like manner he takes to task occupational and business licensing as a bar to minority entry. He observes, for example, how Illinois and Missouri are shown in a study to discriminate against black applicants by requiring them to pass both a written examination and a performance test to qualify for a license as a beautician. He argues that the written exam tends to screen out minority people on the basis of characteristics unrelated to job performance.

Similarly, he observes that the cost of a license to operate a taxi in places like New York, Boston, Philadelphia, and Chicago runs as high as $68,000—quite out of reach for a typical citizen, especially a minority one. The result is that few blacks own cabs in those cities. In Washington, D.C., however, where there is no restrictive taxi licensing, black taxicab ownership is relatively high. Further, Washington taxi service is more frequent and less expensive than in the taxi-licensing cities, notes Dr. Williams. He asks economic educators to take note of this.

In their own way each of our contributors points up the significance of economic education. That significance is essentially two-fold in nature: First, economic education confronts the real world of scarcity, of how man earns a living, of the critical role of choices or "trade-offs" for young and old alike both in their citizenship roles and their economic roles as producers and consumers. Hence, the desirability if not essentiality of an economic education program at the secondary level, if not, ideally, at the secondary *and* elementary levels—K–12.

Second, I believe the Burkett Miller lecturers are saying that economics as a social science is anything but dull and boring—if properly taught. According to Drs. Hansen and Kourilsky, an economic education program can have enriching effects on such other school studies as math, reading, and history. Dr. Kourilsky shows that in her experience-based program students actually show a more positive attitude toward school and learning.

The contributors are also largely of the opinion that economics is not without a degree of controversy, involving different schools of thought and different viewpoints—those of corporations, unions, farm groups, consumer organizations, and partisan politicians. This situation may pose a problem for the economic educator. But if that educator accepts that situation and hews to economics as a science and to principle and fact, he or she can instill more zest and drama into the course and is likely to be more successful in the classroom mission.

Certainly school administrators and teachers are getting increasing pressure to include economics in the school curriculum. As Dr. Oliverio noted, some two dozen states require instruction in economics at the secondary level, with some states featuring a K-12 program. Some states call for consumer economics, some for career economics. And some states indicate that the economics should be along the lines of the free enterprise system. Tennessee is a case in point, and its mandate reads as follows:

49-1928. Instruction on free enterprise system in public high schools.
The state board of education shall establish a program of instruction for the public high schools on the essentials of the free enterprise system. Instruction shall be given in accordance with the course of study prescribed by the state board of education for at least one (1) semester, equal to one half (½) unit of credit. The state board of education shall prescribe suitable teaching material for such instruction.
As used in this section, "instruction on the essentials of the free enterprise system," may be construed to include a minimum of thirty (30) weeks participation in the Junior Achievement Program, and such participation shall render the student eligible for the one half (½) unit of credit granted under this section.
As used in this section "free enterprise" means an economic system characterized by private or corporate ownership of capital goods, by investments that are determined by private decision rather than by state control, and by prices, production, and the distribution of goods that are determined in a free manner.
[Act 1974 (Adj. S.), Ch. 485, Sec. 1.]

Such state mandates are one thing; teacher training to meet these mandates is another. A survey of teacher qualifications in Tennessee, conducted by the Center for Economic Education at the University of Tennessee at Chattanooga, indicates that a considerable number of economics and social studies teachers have had little or no training in economics.⁶ There is a good chance that this situation holds for some other states as well.

Fortunately there is an organization specifically created to reduce economic illiteracy by improving the quality and increasing the quantity of economics taught in our schools—by *trained* teachers using the most effective teaching materials. This nonprofit, nonpartisan educational organization is the Joint Council on Economic Education. Headquartered in New York, the Joint Council has helped spawn a network of state-affiliated councils which work directly with state departments of education and local school systems.

The Joint Council and its 49 state affiliates, such as the Tennessee Council on Economic Education, sponsor teacher workshops, institutes, and in-service programs designed to upgrade teacher training in economic education. These workshops, institutes, and in-service programs also help teachers and school administrators to develop materials and techniques for building economic understanding in the classroom.

Most of these teacher training programs are based at college and university centers for economic education. (The UTC Center for Economic Education is an example.) These centers are usually authorized to grant certification and matriculation credit to teachers, thus giving them an added incentive to pursue economic education courses and increase their teaching skills in economics. There are currently more than 200 Centers for Economic Education in the country, with some 500 cooperating school districts, enrolling over nine million students.⁷ Teachers and school administrators interested in securing economic education training should contact their local Center for Economic Education or State Council on Economic Education, usually headquartered in the state capital.

With these thoughts, this book is commended to the reader as *Economic Education: Investing in the Future*. The reader will not find here a history of efforts to establish economic education programs, a cross-cultural or cross-national compari-

---

⁶A copy of an analysis of this survey is available on request from the UTC Center for Economic Education, Chattanooga, Tenn., 37402.

⁷See Joint Council on Economic Education, Annual Report for Fiscal Year Ended June 30, 1980, p. 4.

son of economic education, a discussion of the employee economic education movement and other phases of economic education. But some appropriate sources are indicated in the brief bibliography to this chapter. What he will find here is the case for economic education, including its ways and means, its problems and opportunities. After all, the young shall inherit the earth. Best that they be prepared, in terms of economic education and otherwise.

Brief Bibliography
General Reference Materials

Campbell, Sally R. (ed.) *Our Economic System*. Chicago: Sears, Roebuck, 1976. Free. Out of print.
  A short 63-page booklet consisting of twelve essays sponsored by the Business Roundtable, which originally appeared in *Reader's Digest*. A multi-disciplinary teachers' guide accompanies each essay, expanding on key concepts and involving students in economic decision-making as it relates to their roles as consumers, producers, and citizens.
Hansen, W. Lee; Bach, G. L.; Calderwood, James D.; and Saunders, Phillip. *A Framework for Teaching Economics: Basic Concepts—Part I*. New York: Joint Council on Economic Education, 1977. $2.50.
  First in a two-part publication entitled *Master Curriculum Guide in Economics for the Nation's Schools*. This framework of basic concepts will provide the most complete, workable guideline for planning curricula for the teaching of economic education.

Methods Materials

Dawson, George G. (ed.) *Economic Education Experiences of Enterprising Teachers: Volume 1*. New York: Joint Council on Economic Education, 1972. $2.00.
  Chapters 4 and 5 of this manual particularly deal with effective teaching techniques that can be used in high school economics, along with new approaches to teaching Government in conjunction with Economics. Also includes lists of textbooks and other readings, audio-visuals, and games.
Joyce, Bruce R. *New Strategies for Social Education*. Chicago: Science Research Associates, Inc., 1972. $10.95.
  Chapter 4 includes a "systems approach" to the study of economic systems, in which real-life situations are used to teach concepts.

Prehn, Edward C. *Teaching High School Economics.* New York: New York City Council on Economic Education, 1976. $5.95.

Designed to aid the high school teacher looking for an introduction to the teaching of economics. Included are discussion techniques, teaching strategies, lesson planning, and use of the problems approach. Chapters 12 and 13 in particular deal with effective teaching techniques for the slow learner. Also included are behavioral aims, the inquiry approach, and methods for making economics come alive for the inner city student. Materials on simulation games, the use of the community as a laboratory, mini-courses, and similar devices are prominently treated.

Employee Economic Education

Emanuel, Myron; Snodgrass, Curtis; Gildea, Joyce; Rosenberg, Karn. *Corporate Economic Education Programs: An Evaluation and Appraisal.* New York: Financial Executives Research Foundation, 1979. $5.95.

A number of U.S. firms have initiated economic education programs as part of their social responsibility function and to help maintain support of the free enterprise system. Many constituencies—employees, shareholders, students, and community organizations—are recipients of the programs. Business firms and concerned individuals are trying hard to reach these traditional "grass roots" groups in order to gain support for the free enterprise system. This 400-page study addresses the content, goals, and evaluation of these programs, as well as suggestions for businesses that wish to initiate or improve their programs.

University of Southern California Center for the Study of Private Enterprise. *Employee Economic Information Program: A Procedures Guide.* Los Angeles: USC, June 1980, 7th Revision. $5.

Chapter I provides an overview of how to implement an Employee Economic Information Program, including an employee survey questionnaire, information on an ongoing program, the small business program, questions most frequently asked by persons interested in starting an employee program, and some helpful hints offered by those who have conducted effective programs. Chapter II provides program media which can be used with little or no modification. The start-up program contents focus on six topics; materials for each topic are provided which consist of posters, payroll envelope stuffers, brainteasers and puzzles, and articles for company newsletters. Chapter III provides supplementary program media, including information on small group meetings, audio-visual materials, other ideas, brief notes on recent books, and useful resource directories that may be helpful to program directors.

I

Economic Education and America's Love-Hate Affair with Business

by G. L. Bach

The typical American has long both admired and mistrusted big business and the men and women who run it. There is almost a vacillating love-hate affair between them. The causes are many and complex, and a better understanding of the role of business in today's economy will depend in large part on what business itself does and how it does it. But better economic education also has a role, and with the two together we can reasonably hope for improvement in the level of understanding that is now so painfully low and uneven.

President Coolidge is said to have observed, back in the Roaring Twenties, "The business of America is business." And in those days, the business of America *was* business. Everyone admired America's great factories, our efficient production lines, our ever-ascending stock market. Henry Ford was perhaps the best known American in the Western world, and perhaps the most admired.

Indeed, over the century and a half from its establishment to 1929, America provided a warm, welcoming environment for business, for individual initiative and a market-oriented economy. The British, French, and American revolutions that gave us political democracy provided the ideological framework for economic individualism. Political democracy and modern private enterprise economics arose in the same historical setting, part of the same broad sweep of history.

Individual freedom and self-interest were at the core of this revolution. In politics every man should be free to vote as he pleased—to look out for his own interests at the ballot box. In economic life, every man should be free to seek his own self-interest—to work where he wished and to spend his money on whatever he wanted. Compassion for the poor, the losers in the economic race, was not lacking. But by and large, Americans admired the winners—the successful businessman, the skilled artisan, the imaginative entrepreneur who somehow managed to found and guide a business that grew and prospered.

The successful businessman was not uniformly admired. The market could be harsh, demanding, cruel. And, indeed, as the 1800's wore on, some successful businessmen seemed to push the limits of acceptable behavior to the margin. The great trusts of the 1800's (in oil, steel, whisky, cordage) concentrated business power to a previously unknown extent, sometimes using that power ruthlessly to drive small businesses over the brink. Human values were relegated to the background as workers were pressed for more efficiency and output, and consumers exploited when strong monopoly positions were achieved.

The American people admired big business and successful big businessmen—but the very democratic spirit that led to the political revolutions of the 1700s led to growing distrust of vast concentrations of economic power, however great their advantages might be in pouring out goods and providing jobs for the masses. One major result was the Sherman Act of 1890, which for the first time spelled out America's determination that most of our economic system should, and would, work competitively.

This is no time to detail the history of antitrust. It is of interest here mainly as a broad socio-economic response to the growing concentration of power. The Sherman Act, and the other antitrust legislation that followed, was a typically American response to excesses—a pragmatic attempt to outlaw what was dangerous while preserving what was beneficial. The Congressional debates on these acts were by-and-large not carefully reasoned intellectual arguments, but rather strong statements of resentment at the unfair practices and abuses of power by John D. Rockefeller and the other great trustmakers. They were for protection for the little man, be he consumer or small businessman. And so it has been throughout history. We Americans are pragmatic people, not given to precisely reasoned theories of the way our nation should work. Nor are our laws often the result of carefully reasoned theoretical analysis.

The year 1929 was the end of an era. Franklin Roosevelt was the leader of a violent attack on big business and what he perceived as its abuses of power. It was a free-swinging, populist attack on concentrations of economic power and on those who would enshrine profits for the wealthy few over concern for the common man. World War II and the immediate post-war years brought business back into the good graces of many Americans. American business was prodigiously successful in producing the weapons of war and in maintaining the high American standard of consumption even with half our total production going to support the war effort. But even then, war profiteering and high prices were widely alleged, and even the prosperity of the 1950s and 1960s could not overcome the widespread doubts about the role of big business in America. It is on those doubts that I would now like to focus attention.

The Love-Hate Syndrome

Public opinion polls over the last few decades on the attitude of Americans toward big business show a clear picture. The American public believes that free enterprise made this country great; that when business makes good profits, the country prospers; and that business brings better products and good jobs to the people. America is for private enterprise, not socialism. In the annual Louis Harris Survey for 1966, 80 percent or more of all Americans polled expressed these views, and similar results have been reported by all the other polls.

But at the same time, similar majorities said that business is too self-interested and spends too much time trying to make profits, not enough helping to solve the nation's problems—depressions, the central cities, poverty, race prejudice, and pollution. Business has vast power, which can be used either for good or ill, the public feels, and that power is focused too exclusively on trying to make profits.

I have constructed a little table based mainly on the Harris Surveys, showing how many of the American people had "a great deal of confidence" in major social institutions, including big business and their leaders between 1966 and 1976, a period encompassing much of the Vietnam War and Watergate. In

1966, 72 percent expressed great confidence in medicine and in science, 62 percent in the military, 61 percent in higher education, 42 percent in Congress, only 22 percent in organized labor. How about "big business"? 55 percent. Not bad.

Table *Confidence of the American Public in Major Social Institutions: Percentage Reporting "a Great Deal of Confidence"*[1]

	1966	1976
1. Medicine	72%	42%
2. The military	62	23
3. Higher educational institutions	61	44
4. Major companies	55	16
5. Press	29	22
6. Congress	42	9
7. Organized labor	22	10

[1] Based mainly on Louis Harris and Associates, Inc. polls. Results for different polls are not precisely comparable because of slight changes in questions. Similar results are shown by other polls.

But ten years later (in 1976), all these figures had nosedived. The public had clearly lost confidence in *all* major institutions. The table tells the story. But big business took almost the biggest slide of all—from 55 to only 16 percent.

Why? The polls do not give an answer, although they suggest some possible causes. One could argue—I do—that there was a massive loss of confidence in all our major social institutions during that painful decade. The divisive Vietnam War, Watergate, and the massive tumult at home undoubtedly accounted for a big part of the loss, but by no means all of it.

More basically, Americans have always mistrusted bigness and concentrated power, and distrust built up rapidly during this decade. The massive bribes paid by American businessmen at home and abroad further undercut America's faith in big business and its leaders. Consumerism, led by Ralph Nader, scored tellingly on many occasions—shoddy products, pollution, bribery, discrimination. Certainly many of Nader's claims were excessive and unfair, and some were effectively rebutted. But the overall impact was painful indeed for big business. To many Americans, Nader's allegations merely confirmed what they had long suspected about the powerful heads of the great corporations.[1]

What is this business power that the public resents and fears? The answer clearly varies from time to time. Monopoly is a persistent worry, but not the main one, if we are to judge from the pollsters. If you ask people today, "What is bad about big corporations?," chances are the answers will include polluting the environment, selling shoddy products, and overcharging people.

I suspect that, underlying these, is resentment and fear of the concentrated power of any immense, monolithic institution, over which people feel they have no real control. How shall I protest to General Electric if I buy a "lemon," or to the government if I object to its policies in South Africa? This growing impotence may help account for the big drop in confidence in the government and labor unions, as well as big business. It may be a more basic cause than any actual misdeeds by big business, and certainly than businesses' failure to produce good products at reasonable costs—what Adam Smith said is their main job.

Strikingly, the public is much more friendly toward little business than big business, even though by the test of the market big business often does a better job. Again, the fact that the average American knows personally the little businessman and his problems, may help to account for this difference in attitude. The impersonal giant corporation is very impersonal indeed. Its president is a name that receives a six-figure salary, not a human being whose children have measles and crises like the rest of us, or the owner of the local mom and pop grocery. Americans' support for a "private enterprise system" has remained firm even so. But there is no way one can look at these opinion poll figures without recognizing the painful fact that the public doesn't understand, or like very well, the big business firms that are the backbone of our present economic system, especially in the manufacturing and financial sectors.

Nor are the results noted above to be brushed aside as "merely polls." The last decade has seen an unparalleled flood of govern-

---

[1]For a more detailed analysis, see S. M. Lipset and W. Schneider, "How's Business? What the Public Thinks," *Public Opinion*, July 1978.

ment regulations of nearly every aspect of business. The typical American may be deeply distrustful of big government too, but when he is unhappy with business and its practices, his first instinct is to turn to the government to "do something about it."

In a recent study for the Joint Economic Committee, Murray Weidenbaum reports that 20,036 pages were required in the Federal Register in 1970 to list the new laws and regulations applicable to businesses. By 1977 this had increased to an horrendous 65,603 pages. The administrative costs alone of 41 federal regulatory agencies totalled $4.5 billion in 1978, and a rough estimate of the costs incurred by business firms in complying was about $100 billion.[2] The power of the public over business is political as well as economic.

The Case for a Market-Directed System

The case *for* a private enterprise, market-directed system is a complex, sophisticated one. It is that each of us, seeking his own self-interest, will produce the greatest good for all of us when this self-interest is channeled into meeting consumers' demands by sellers' competition in the marketplace. Such a system, it can be argued, will give us maximum efficiency in the allocation of our scarce resources to meet human wants, rapid progress in producing more of what we want, and, perhaps most important of all, wide dispersion of economic power so that no individual or institution has more than a tiny amount of influence over what is produced, how, and who gets it.[3] It is a powerful case, once understood, but one that seems to many people intuitively implausible and unconvincing.

By contrast, the case *against* the private enterprise, market-oriented system is simple and direct. It is that if we let each person pursue his own selfish interests, some will win the race, and these rich and powerful winners will seize more and more of

---

[2] *The Costs of Government Regulation of Business*, Joint Economic Committee, United States Congress, April 10, 1978.

[3] More rigorously put, economists call this Pareto optimality. It would not assure the best of all possible worlds, but would produce an efficient use of our scarce resources in which no change could improve anyone's lot without worsening someone else's.

what is produced for themselves, leaving less and less for the powerless members of society. Profit, in this argument, is a rip-off by the capitalist rich from the worker-consumer-poor— unlike the argument *for* a market-directed system, where profits are the carrot that leads businessmen to produce what consumers most want, and the basis for investment in new factories to produce more next year.

It is no wonder that relatively few people understand the case for a private-enterprise, market-oriented economy. It does not sound plausible to a lot of people that in trying to maximize their own profits, businesses will in fact help others. Nor are the conditions under which markets "fail" intuitively obvious. Yet understanding these "market failures" is essential to real understanding of the market system.

Such is the problem facing economic education in our society. It is not that business is good and unions or consumer groups bad. On the contrary, it is that all can participate together in a competitive economic system that will best serve their combined individual interests. Nor is it correct to suppose, or teach others, that the case for a private enterprise market-oriented economy brooks no role for government or for other economic institutions in our society. Understanding involves just that— understanding, not propaganda in favor of one or another of our economics groups or institutions. Even the most ardent private-enterprise economists recognize the need for government intervention to protect contracts and property rights; to assure competition among sellers and buyers; to correct for externalities which are not picked up by market cost calculations; to improve the mobility of resources in our society; to produce public goods like the court system and national defense; and, lastly, to redistribute incomes *if* we as a people collectively decide that is what we want to do.

Agreeing on how much government intervention is necessary or desirable is not easy. But any rational discussion must be based on an understanding of how the economy works. Economic education consists of helping people to understand the issues so they can make up their own minds rationally. As Professor Hansen says in Chapter II, economics is a way of thinking about problems, a set of analytical tools to help people think straight about them, and an orderly way of applying those tools to the economic problems we face. It is not propaganda, not cant. It is profoundly democratic in the sense that each individual must make up his own mind as to what is best for him and best for the whole society.

We desperately need more economic education. Most Americans are abysmally ignorant about both the facts of the American mixed private enterprise system and the intellectual case for it. Businessmen are especially upset by the fact that Americans repeatedly believe profits are 30 or 40 percent of sales, rather than the 5 percent they average for the whole economy. Businessmen should be upset by this. But they should be even more upset at the failure of the public to understand what the real functions of profits are—and at their own failure to have made the case effectively.

Economic Understanding and Attitudes Toward Business

I have argued that if we are to make intelligent decisions about our economic system, and the roles of business in it, we must understand in at least an elementary way how the system works. So is ignorance the reason for the widespread mistrust of big business?

I think it is one important reason, and we should be doing a lot more about it. But it's not the only reason. Two distinguished American businessmen, leaders of two large business firms, and a well-known university professor, suggest that business has itself to blame in no small way. J. Irwin Miller, chairman of the Cummins Engine Company, said in a recent speech:

> American businessmen today are indignant. They are having troubles with profit margins, troubles with government regulators, troubles with labor demands, troubles with foreign governments. On top of all this, anti-business sentiment is growing. It is unfair, we businessmen tell ourselves. Nobody . . . gives us credit for the great contribution of business to the nation and to the world . . . To all this, my reply, as a business manager of more than 40 years service, is "Down Boy!"
>
> We had better ask ourselves a hard question or two. A few weeks ago the papers reported that 430 corporations had disclosed to the IRS that they had made a variety of illegal political and other payments in the

recent past. We have all read about ... housing development scandals, security frauds, doctors ripping off Medicare ...

When your wife confronts you, therefore, indignant about the quality of some merchandise she bought, the way she was treated at the store, the plumber's bill for fixing something that still doesn't work ... blame not the socialistic college professor for her anger, blame the performance of the American businesses with which she has to deal.[4]

About the same time, writing in the *New York Times*, Thomas A. Murphy, chairman of the General Motors Corporation, the world's largest manufacturing business, wrote in much the same vein:

> We must compete for the public favor where this favor is to be won, in the crucial interface of business with the customer, in the myriad one-on-one encounters between buyers and seller which take place every day ... If we in business want to remain as free as we still are to respond to the desires of our customers rather than to those of the government regulators, we are going to have to fulfill the businessman's first, last, and always responsibility—the responsibility to satisfy those customers today, not tomorrow.[5]

Both Messrs. Murphy and Miller know that many charges against big business are unfair, that one highly visible mistake may outweigh hundreds of cases of efficient service. But their frank advice to their fellow businessmen underscores a fundamental truth—what business does speaks louder than what it says!

Professor Irving Kristol, writing in the *Wall Street Journal* at the time of the OPEC oil crisis in 1974, posed the problem sharply:

> Every day, in every way, the large corporation looks more and more like a species of dinosaur on its lumbering way to extinction ... The large corporation used to be a single-purpose institution; an economic institution directed toward economic growth. It was very good at this job ... But its very size and importance have resulted in its job assignment being changed ... The large corporation's executives have to learn to think politically, as well as economically. That is the price of bigness and power.[6]

---

[4]From "Business and the Arts," address by J. Irwin Miller, chairman, Cummins Engine Co., June 21, 1977.
[5]*New York Times*, Oct. 10, 1976.
[6]*Wall Street Journal*, Feb. 14, 1974.

But, he argues, they have not learned to think politically. Following the OPEC oil embargo, for example, the giant oil companies took huge profits from higher prices, and raised both dividends and executive salaries. How better to have demonstrated their unconcern for the public's welfare, with their dominant focus on profits? Had they been "thinking politically," Kristol asks, would they not have foregone some of those profits, dividends and salaries? Surely they would have realized that they had another and more important task than raising profits—securing the trust and good will of the public. And this second mission, since it is the precondition of survival, must have priority over the first. Large corporations, Kristol wrote, have shown little evidence of capacity to adapt to a rapidly changing environment and changing public expectations of how they can best serve society.

The Need for Legitimacy

All social institutions must have legitimacy if they are to prosper. Legitimacy comes mostly from a widely-shared feeling that the institution is doing a useful job for society, and doing it well. And it is on this source that business, and indeed the whole private-enterprise, market-directed system, must largely rely for their legitimacy. All other sources (shared defense against external threat, as in war; age and venerability; mystery and symbolism, as in religion) are either irrelevant or of dubious usefulness to business and the market system.

During the first century and a half of America's history, business, profits, and the market system generally had high legitimacy. But legitimacy is precarious. The Great Depression of the 30s and the complex mix of Vietnam, Watergate, and the collapse of the national morale over the past decade, have seriously eroded big businesses' legitimacy.

In order to rebuild its legitimacy, big business will have to face up to the need to better meet the public's expectations for it, even if this involves going well beyond short-run profit maximization. Kristol, though one may object to his examples, is surely right that big business today is a social and political institution, perhaps as much as an economic one, and the tests of legitimacy will be broader than the short-run test of the "bottom line," as businessmen are fond of calling the total profit figure.

My files are full of corporate policy statements from businesses attempting to identify and live up to standards of conduct for constructive and profitable performance in the modern economy. I commend them. But businessmen will gain little support merely by proclaiming that their main job is to make profits. The public is not deeply moved by General Motors' or Exxon's proclaimed need for more profit when it is announcing annual profits of billions of dollars annually.[7] Business's main job is to serve the public well by producing what the public wants at reasonable prices, and providing steady jobs at reasonable pay. The case for profits is that they are the most effective incentive we know for getting business's job done efficiently, and for accumulating capital, and not that business has some God-given right to them.

Here we are back at economic education again. Without at least elementary public understanding of the way the system works, business will have a difficult time making its case and the case for capitalism. Only more economic education and business words *and* deeds together are likely to provide the legitimacy so essential to business firms if they are to play their role effectively at the center of a market-oriented economy.

To expect universal admiration to replace the present ambivalence in America's love-hate relationship with big business is to be naïve indeed. But constructive steps are there to be taken. The new program which these papers introduce here at the University of Tennessee at Chattanooga is an example of constructive action for the benefit of business and all of us.

[7]Recessions can sharply change this picture. For example, General Motors reported a combined loss of some $1 billion for the second and third quarters of 1980—Ed.

II

Are Americans Economically Literate? An Appraisal

by W. Lee Hansen

The phrase "economic literacy" crops up with increasing frequency in news reports, commentaries, and public discussions, reflecting a growing concern about the lack of economic understanding among Americans, particularly among young Americans. My intention is to explore the subject of economic literacy—and hence its corollary of economic education—by focusing on these five questions:
—Why is economic literacy important?
—What do we mean by economic literacy?
—What do people know about economics?
—Why don't people know more than they do?
—What can be done to improve people's understanding of economics?

Why Is Economic Literacy Important?

The causes of the recent concern about economic literacy are several, and the responses to them have taken various forms. The 1976 Bicentennial offered an opportunity few could resist to reexamine various facets of American society and experience, particularly its economic system. This opportunity was heightened because the Bicentennial also marked the 200th anniversary of the publication of *The Wealth of Nations*. This book was written by Adam Smith, a Scotsman, who is widely regarded as the father of modern economics. As a result, we witnessed a number of efforts to explore the strengths and weaknesses of the American economic system.

More important without doubt was the emergence in the

1970s of a growing number of vexing and complex economic problems with impacts on wide segments of society. Illustrative of these problems are double-digit inflation, slower economic growth, sharply increased unemployment, higher oil prices, ever increasing government regulation, and pressure for more economic planning.

The reexamination of the economic system, combined with the emergence of these new problems, heightened the belief that many people lacked sufficient understanding of economics to deal intelligently and effectively with these problems. This belief was strengthened by such studies and surveys as the Advertising Council's[1] which documented wide gaps in people's knowledge of economics. Ours, after all, is a democracy—the presence of too many economic illiterates could well lead to faulty public policy, if it hasn't already. Widespread economic understanding seems to be a must in a free society where the rule of one-person-one-vote prevails.

Happily, new efforts to enhance economic literacy have begun—including several by the business sector. For example, in 1975 the Advertising Council launched a substantial program to educate people about economics. It began a comprehensive advertising campaign, mass distribution of a booklet on the American economy, and dissemination of other educational materials such as films. The Business Roundtable sponsored a series of advertisements in *The Reader's Digest*[2] to inform readers about the American economic system. The National Association of Manufacturers conducted an "educational" campaign to tell the public about the economic system and the role of government in that system. In addition, many businesses advertised in newspapers and magazines in an effort to inform readers about how the economic system operates.

Another response to economic illiteracy came from the publishing industry. The weekly newsmagazines and national newspapers all expanded their economics coverage and attempted to reduce the complexities in an effort to help people under-

---

[1] *Ad Council Economic Communicator,* a publication of the Advertising Council, Inc., New York, May 1976, March 1977.
[2] *Reader's Digest,* Jan. 1975–July 1975.

stand economics. And some of our best economics journalists sought to unveil the mysteries of economics, with such books as *Understanding the Economy: For People Who Can't Stand Economics*[3] by Alfred Malabre Jr. of the *Wall Street Journal* and *Economics in Plain English: All You Need to Know About Economics in Language Anyone Can Understand*[4] by Leonard Silk of the *New York Times*.

The TV and film industries collaborated, producing the John Kenneth Galbraith TV series, *The Age of Uncertainty*[5]; the popular TV program *Wall Street Week*; a series of films on American economic history (supported by Phillips Petroleum); a film on Adam Smith (supported by the Liberty Fund); a seven-film series, *The People on Market Street* (Walt Disney); a 15-program series called *Trade-Offs* (Joint Council on Economic Education); and most recently the Public Broadcasting System presentation of the Milton Friedman series, *Free to Choose*.

New responses were also apparent among economic educators. In the early 1970s there had already been a flowering of innovative textbooks for teaching elementary economics at the college level. The Joint Council on Economic Education was proceeding with its development of a *Master Curriculum Guide* to help improve pre-college economics instruction.[6] The National Science Foundation supported a major conference in early 1976 on new directions in economic education.[7] The Joint Council on Economic Education was also hard at work develop-

---

[3] Alfred Malabre, Jr., *Understanding the Economy: For People Who Can't Stand Economics*, New York: Dodd, Mead, 1976.

[4] Leonard Silk, *Economics in Plain English: All You Need to Know About Economics in Language Anyone Can Understand*, New York: Simon & Schuster, 1978.

[5] Based loosely on the Galbraith book, *The Age of Uncertainty*. Boston: Houghton-Mifflin, 1978.

[6] W. Lee Hansen, G. L. Bach, James D. Calderwood, and Phillip Saunders, *Master Curriculum Guide, A Framework for Teaching Economics: Basic Concepts*, New York: Joint Council on Economic Education, 1977.

[7] W. Lee Hansen and Donald R. Wentworth, *Perspectives on Economic Education, A Report on Conference Proceedings*, a report on the National Conference on Needed Research and Development in Precollege Economic Education held Feb. 12–14, 1976, in New Orleans, and funded by the National Science Foundation.

ing a Teacher Training Program to facilitate the acquisition of instructional skills by economics graduate students.[8]

To sum up, new concerns were met by new responses, responses from the private and the nonprofit sectors of the economy, supported by the efforts of concerned economists and economic educators. It is too early to assess the fruits of these various efforts, but we trust that evaluations of them will be forthcoming in the near future.

What Do We Mean By Economic Literacy?

The term "economic literacy" may sound like a cliché but its wide use demands that it be discussed here. Where did the term come from? It probably crept into our vocabulary during the 1960s, most likely in connection with publication of a special report on economic education in the schools by the National Task Force on Economic Education in 1961.[9] That report did not use the term literacy; rather it employed the phrase "economic understanding" to describe the economic knowledge necessary for effective citizenship by the average high school graduate.

Other than the Task Force Report, one finds little help in searching for a definition of the term economic literacy. Textbooks often cite "literacy" as one of their goals, but in nonoperational terms. Some texts have been more specific, stating as their objective, for example, the development of students' ability to be more effective and critical readers of newspaper articles about economics. But again, the terms "critical" and "effective" are so ill-defined that outsiders, and perhaps even the student readers, have difficulty knowing exactly what is meant. In short, no definition exists that provides a meaning for, much less a way of measuring, economic literacy.

Rather than belaboring the point, we should search for another term. Literacy has too much of an all-or-nothing connotation anyway. We might be better off thinking of some kind

---

[8]Phillip Saunders, Arthur L. Welsh, and W. Lee Hansen (eds.), *Resource Manual for Teacher Training Programs in Economics*, New York: Joint Council on Economic Education, 1978.

[9]Committee for Economic Development, *Economic Education in the Schools: Report of the National Task Force on Economic Education*, 1961.

of a continuum of knowledge, ranging from no knowledge all the way to the professional economist's knowledge. Again, we find difficulties with words; the word "knowledge" may be too strong because it implies truth or falsity. Perhaps, to borrow from Kenneth Boulding, former president of the American Economic Association, we would be better advised to think of people's "images" or "perceptions" of economics. People learn through experience, including schooling, and as they learn, their images or perceptions change. These images and perceptions vary widely, depending on the nature of one's experience. The images and perceptions—or knowledge—of professional economists tend to be very elaborate, whereas those of the ordinary citizen have a "folk" quality to them.

Thus, the object of economic education, it would seem, is to move people away from "folk" to more "elaborate" knowledge, in the hope of changing people's images and perceptions about economics.

What Do People Know?

It is not easy to determine what people know about economics. Economic understanding requires various kinds of knowledge, such as concepts and how to apply them, analytical skills, some institutional knowledge, and an ability to weigh alternatives. The difficulties are compounded because in dealing with all human endeavors the value judgments of individuals invariably come to bear. It is not clear that we are yet able to assess people's ability to combine all these elements, but we do have various instruments and methods to assess some dimensions of this knowledge. The first volume of the Joint Council on Economic Education's *Master Curriculum Guide*, offers one method of bringing together these elements.[10]

To determine the effects of formal instruction in economics, several tests have been devised, such as the *Test of Economic Literacy* for junior high school grades, *Test of Economic Understanding* for high school grades, and *Test of Understanding College Economics* for college students. All of these

[10]Hansen, et al., *Master Curriculum Guide*.

tests attempt to measure school-taught economics. A few of the conclusions drawn from the results of these tests are worth mentioning.
- The scores of males exceed those of females, except at the lower grades.
- High school and college economics courses increase scores significantly.
- Courses have lasting effects, because knowledge is retained five years after college instruction.
- Retention is enhanced for those people whose job experience is closely related to economics.

There are other tests that attempt to measure what people know about economics, whether or not they have done formal coursework. The National Assessment of Educational Progress still does not include enough economics questions to give a good reading on the economics knowledge of students or of young adults (age 26–35). The College Entrance Examination Board's "CLEP" provide a means for students to demonstrate the economics knowledge they have acquired in high school or informally, with the possibility of obtaining college credit if their knowledge is sufficient. And in 1978 the Educational Testing Services made available, as part of its Career Skills Assessment Program, a test of *Personal Economics Skills* that deserves to be examined.

At least two important surveys were undertaken recently to find out what adults know about economics. One, a survey sponsored by the Business Roundtable in 1975, turned up several interesting results:
- Adults with economics courses exhibited more knowledge than those without economics courses;
- Male scores exceeded those of females;
- The more schooling people had, the better was their knowledge of economics.[11]

The other, a detailed survey in 1974 sponsored by the Advertising Council, concluded: "Economic understanding of the American public is incomplete and fragmentary. Few adults are

---

[11]Research Group, Business Roundtable's Public Information Committee, Corporate Marketing Research Section, DuPont Co., 1975.

highly informed and few are totally uninformed. Even among the best educated groups and those directly involved in the human world, there are deficiencies in information though they are smaller in degree."[12] The survey also revealed that most people's knowledge came from their personal experiences. At the same time, most people saw their role in the economic system as a passive one.

Any assessment of what people know requires that we have a broader base of data and preferably one that permits comparisons over time. One source of such information is public opinion polls that have over the years sought out people's responses to a wide array of questions. Typically, these questions concern real-world issues and problems rather than textbook learning. Contrary to what many might expect, these polls do sample more than opinion; they ask for facts and at times for analysis that reflects economic reasoning. Nevertheless, there is often a blending of knowledge with attitudes or opinions which confuses matters. Despite this difficulty, what can we learn from these survey results?

A review of the public opinion surveys reveals that they provide seven types of potentially useful information:

1. Surveys ask for facts. The only question at issue for us is the importance of these facts and to what extent they reflect the knowledge required for economic literacy.

2. They ask for assessments of the most important problems currently facing the economy. The answers reflect what is uppermost in people's minds, including such concerns as inflation and unemployment. Regardless of how people reach their conclusions, the answers provide a measure of the perceived impact of economic forces on them.

3. Surveys ask for assessments about the future of the economy over the coming months or years. Because the accuracy of these judgments can be determined later, it is possible to ascertain how well the respondents understand the working of the economic system. Of course, we must remember that the accuracy of the forecasts of professional economists leaves something

---

[12]Compton Advertising, Inc., *National Survey on the American Economic System*, New York: Advertising Council, Inc., 1975.

to be desired, and hence caution must be used in interpreting these assessments.

4. Surveys ask what actions are necessary to deal with specific economic problems. For some of these questions there may be no clear consensus view even among economists. Where there is a consensus view, we can determine whether the respondents' views agree with the conventional wisdom of economists.

5. Surveys ask how people would behave under certain specified conditions. The answers can be dismissed with the criticism that they reflect self-interest; however, there is nothing wrong with viewing economic literacy as including an awareness of one's self-interest. But these answers can also indicate how individuals may be swayed by considerations of public interest. For example, a presidential speech calling for individual sacrifices justified for the common good may or may not be effective.

6. Surveys ask about priorities—"what ought to be" questions. These clearly reflect individual value judgments, colored by the surrounding events.

7. Surveys ask about people's attitudes toward the economic system and its effectiveness. These responses also are likely to reflect value judgments.

From these seven types of questions what can we learn about the public's knowledge of economics or its economic understanding? Questions 1, 3, 4, and 5 have potential value in assessing economic literacy. It is obvious that questions 6 and 7 are not informative because they address normative questions. Question 2 is ambiguous because of the difficulty of knowing what influences the responses—some positive analysis of "what is" or a normative evaluation of "what ought to be." Whether these will in fact be useful depends heavily on how the questions are worded and what alternative responses are provided.

Let us look at examples of several of these questions to indicate what they can reveal.[13]

---

[13]Readers should consult the following publications for more specific information on the numerous survey results that are presented in the remaining paragraphs of this section of the paper. See *Gallup Opinion Index*, *The Gallup Poll*, *Opinion Research Corporation Public Opinion Index 33*, Princeton: American Institute of Public Opinion and *The Harris Survey*, Chicago: *Chicago Tribune*.

Factual Knowledge   Several recent polls show that many Americans remain grossly ignorant of the most basic facts about the economy. For example, the general public is far off the mark in its knowledge of profit rates. As indicated in an earlier chapter, when asked to estimate the average rate of profit after taxes on sales in American business, the median response has ranged between 30 and 40 percent in recent years. In a more detailed 1975 survey, the estimate of profits for all business was 33 percent, for oil companies 61 percent, and for automobile firms 39 percent. By contrast, 1974 *actual* profit rates on sales averaged 5.2 percent for all business, 7.2 percent for oil companies, and 1.9 percent for automobile firms. The belief that profit rates were so high undoubtedly led 55 percent of the public to state that government should impose a limit on profit levels.

If the ignorance of the general public seems appalling, college students are not much better informed. In a 1975 poll of college students, their median estimate of the profit rate for large national corporations was 45 percent. Interestingly, the median estimate of a "fair profit" was 25 percent. Presumably these are estimates of profits on sales and also after-tax, although this is not fully clear from the wording of the questions. In any case, when asked about the income tax rate on corporate earnings, students estimated a 15 percent figure; the actual tax rate is closer to 50 percent.

These are only a few of the many examples that could be cited showing how little is known about the fundamentals of economics—not only by the general public but also by our future leaders: college students.

Assessment of the State of the Economy   A regularly asked question is: What do you think is the most important problem facing this country today? Many problems—not just economic problems—are listed, and people are allowed to cite more than one problem.

The survey results over the past four years are illuminating. In January 1974 the energy crisis led with 46 percent, high cost of living was second with 25 percent, and unemployment was sixth with 5 percent. By September 1974, at the time of President Ford's Inflation Summit meeting, the high cost of living received an 81 percent response; meanwhile, concerns about unemployment and the energy crisis had almost disappeared. By February 1975, as the recession became apparent, a substantial shift occurred: the cost of living dropped to 60 percent, unemployment rose to 20 percent, and the energy crisis tied for third at 7 percent. Subsequently, concern about unemployment rose steadily to hit a high of 39 percent in March 1977 when unemployment was reaching abnormally high levels. Though concern about inflation had lessened over the intervening period, it was up again to 58 percent in March 1977. Meanwhile, concern about energy rose again, perhaps because of President Carter's newly announced energy program. But then by April 1978 the high cost of living, after dropping to 30 percent in late 1977, rose to 54 percent in April, to 60 percent in July, and to 75 percent in October 1978. The energy concerns had almost disappeared again by July 1978.

Of course, the greatest concern is typically expressed by those people most affected—unemployment by younger and less-educated people and inflation by older, more-educated people. Overall, however, the degree of concern about emerging economic issues varies only slightly with the level of education. The difference between college and high school graduates tends to be somewhat less than between high school graduates and those who completed elementary school. It is doubtful whether these differences can be attributed to economic education, largely because so little economic education takes place.

Assessment of the Future State of the Economy Another one of the regularly asked questions is whether people think prices will go up faster, as fast, or less fast in the next year than they are now. The data show that from January 1975 through July 1977 the percentage believing prices would rise faster hovered between 20 and 27 percent; by April 1978 it had jumped to 43 percent. This is clear evidence of the rapid buildup in early 1978 of expectations about increased inflation. By July 1978, 74 percent of the respondents thought prices would be rising faster in the next year. These data suggest again the extent to which people are attuned to economic changes, even though their factual knowledge may be weak.

Analysis of Economic Problems and Issues The ability of people to pinpoint the causes of economic problems and their remedies cannot be assessed easily through surveys; on the other hand, no obvious alternative method exists for doing this. What can the polls tell us?

In late September 1974 people were asked to indicate the "chief cause of inflation." Given that economists probably could not agree on the answer to this question, it is interesting to learn what the public thought just after the President's Inflation Summit meeting. They believed the chief culprit was the "wage-price spiral," which is rather vague, followed by poor government planning and government overspending, and then five other reasons which each garnered a few votes. However, 18 percent said they did not know, which could be viewed as a refreshingly honest response! Nevertheless, there were some rather dramatic differences in the responses by level of education. The percent responding "don't know" was inversely related to level of education. I leave it up to you whether this indicates that college graduates or grade school graduates are more knowledgeable. The college-educated group responded more specifically, focusing on "government overspending" and "consumer overspending" and downplaying poor government planning, a response which was typical of people with only a grade school education.

People were more evenly divided in response to a companion question on how to deal with inflation. Price controls and wage-price controls got the largest votes, followed by called-for reductions in government and consumer spending. A third of the respondents offered no solution. Interestingly, the remedy of controls obviously dominates that of reductions in effective demand. In early 1979, well after President Carter's announcement of his voluntary wage-price controls, 54 percent of the public favored mandatory controls, 37 percent favored voluntary controls, and 9 percent were unsure. (It is interesting that economists by and large do not support mandatory or perhaps even voluntary controls.) What does this lack of agreement mean? Lack of economic reasoning on the part of the public? Inability to analyze issues? Or the effect of other considerations which dominate their analysis of controls?

Behavior Under Specified Conditions The difficulties of drawing conclusions from this type of question are well illustrated by results of a recent survey. In July 1978 people were asked which of two situations they would prefer. One situation would be getting a pay increase lower than the rise in the cost of living, but with some assurance that the cost of living was being brought under control. The other situation would be getting a pay increase higher than the cost of living but with no assurance that the cost of living was being brought under control; 68 percent said they would prefer a pay raise less than the cost of living; 24 percent wanted a pay raise greater than the cost of living; and 8 percent were not sure. These results indicate that the public has some awareness of the economy-wide consequences of seeking pay increases greater than the cost of living; they also indicate that people are willing to pay a price for greater price stability, in the form of a certain reduction in real income.

Why Don't People Know More?

We can respond to this question in two ways: one focuses on reasons why people *should* know more; the other tries to use economic analysis to offer an answer.

We can come up with several reasons why people *should* know more. One is that the study of economics is interesting, fun, and satisfies idle curiosity about how the world works. Another is that a knowledge of economics is essential for a democracy because of the importance of individual choices. Still another is that a knowledge of economics can make people better off, perhaps financially, but certainly better able to comprehend the forces affecting their well-being. Unfortunately, all of these reasons can be seen as self-serving, for we economists are the producers and also the suppliers of this knowledge.

A second approach is perhaps more enlightening. From a review of the work in economic education it is apparent that much greater attention has been given to the forces determining the supply rather than the demand for economic knowledge and understanding. For example, there has been great emphasis on enhancing the quantity and quality of teachers who produce economic education, improving the curriculum materials used to produce it, and finding improved methods of teaching economics. Once these problems are overcome, students and the public will be eager to snap up our offerings, or so the story goes.

The fact is, where these ideal conditions are met there appears to be no overabundance of demand for such instruction. Many high schools do not offer economics. At college where it is offered many students never take it, and only a few of those who do, come back for a second course. After college, life is busier as people become occupied with families, jobs, and socializing, and they do not seem to be crying out for more economics in their newspapers, on radio or television. Thus, the problem seems to reside not so much with supply as with the demand side of the market for economic education.

Why isn't the demand for economics knowledge stronger? The profession may be partly to blame because the subject is generally seen as dull, difficult, and too mathematical. We may also have given the impression that such a high level of expertise is required that it is fruitless for people to aspire to any kind of amateur status.

But neither have communities typically exerted strong pressure to provide economics courses. Though several states have recently mandated some form of economics instruction in the high schools, the pressure behind these mandates has not been widespread. And where economics is not mandated, it is likely to be an early and easy candidate for budget-cutting as high schools try to cope with lower enrollments and revenue declines in the 1980s.

More important, student demand also appears to be weak. Students see only minimal benefits from acquiring a knowledge of economics. While this knowledge may be useful in understanding how our economic systems operate and the effects of alternative government policies, the benefits to individuals are likely to be seen as indirect and negligible. Economics instruction which might provide direct benefits to individuals because of its value in personal choicemaking, is often viewed as something else, not economics. The distinction, I am suggesting, could be described as economics for "citizenship" versus economics for "personal choice."

When we consider the time and effort involved in learning "citizenship" economics against the negligible personal benefits that accrue, it is obvious why there is ineffectual demand. This occurs despite society's subsidization of economic education (and schooling in general) in the belief that providing such education will produce social benefits that improve the lot of everyone.

What Can Be Done?

We are faced with several questions. For students, how can we make them understand the indirect benefits that come from economic knowledge for effective citizenship? Or should we perhaps try to provide a larger component of economic knowledge for personal decisionmaking? Is there a way of combining these two elements so as to provide more of both types of knowledge, at little or no additional cost, by using new or different methods of teaching and new or different materials? I believe we must proceed in all of these directions. I believe, for example, that the usefulness of the economic concept of "trade-offs" can be demonstrated at both the personal and societal levels—e.g., a new car or a college education at the personal level, guns or butter at the societal level. But above all we must show students how economics affects their lives in concrete ways.

For adults, we face much the same questions. However, the opportunities for providing formal instruction to adults are greatly reduced. What can we substitute for formal instruction? Better and more economics reporting in newspapers and newsmagazines? More extensive radio and TV coverage of economics? Adult education courses? Newspaper courses? I don't have the answers. If I had to voice a hope, it would probably be for improved communication of economic events and issues in the newspapers and television.

But let me indicate another concern, and this is based as much on my experience as a teacher as an economist. The extent to which we can raise the level of economic literacy depends heavily on the extent to which our students acquire general literacy through the entire school system. Unless students possess the basic learning skills, they will experience great difficulty learning economics. To the best of my knowledge, there has been no systematic study of the kinds of knowledge and skills necessary for achieving economic understanding. Despite this, various skills seem essential: the ability to read, to reason, to perform simple mathematical operations, to interpret graphs and tables, and to have some knowledge about the social-political-economic system.

We have begun only recently to develop methods for learning more about the skills and achievements of our students. Of particular value is the National Assessment of Educational Progress, an ongoing effort to appraise the extent of learning among young people aged 9, 13, 17, and 26–35. The results deserve close study by teachers as well as by economists and economic educators because the picture we see is not encouraging. First, the good news: On average, young people read about as well as the experts had anticipated—not well enough but there have been no precipitous declines in reading ability. Next, the bad news, which is not new: Students' writing skills, by which they customarily demonstrate what they learn, are seriously deficient. The mathematical skills of students also leave much to be desired, particularly in consumer math where young people experience difficulty figuring taxes, balancing a checkbook, and so forth. Their ability to read and interpret graphs, tables, and maps is weak. And, finally, their knowledge in social studies and citizenship is not what it should be.

This brief summary suggests that we are going to experience some difficulty teaching economics at the precollege level as long as the general level of literacy is so low. The conclusion to be drawn, I believe, is that we have an important stake in the general quality of our schools. I also think that we could provide some help by thinking about how to place economics more centrally in the curriculum so that it can serve to develop both general literacy and economic literacy. Too, I think the effective economic educator sees economics not as mundane and humdrum but as exciting matter—as to how man seeks to escape poverty and achieve wellbeing and wealth.

Conclusion

The task of economic education—that of helping people increase their knowledge of economics—is a formidable one. We can be heartened because the growing body of research indicates that economics instruction has a positive effect in enhancing people's knowledge. And as the public opinion data indicate, the level of folk knowledge of economics is gratifying. Yet there is clearly a need for more elaborate knowledge to help sharpen people's images and understanding of economics and our economic system.

We must attack the problem on a variety of fronts. More economics instruction in the schools is essential. So too is more and deeper discussions of economic issues in the press and on TV; more adult education in economics; more demonstration of what an economics education will do for you; and, overall, more active participation by students in the learning process.

These solutions will not come about except through the collaborative effort by economists, economic educators, community leaders, journalists, and others. Each of us must devote time to this task. That is why it is so gratifying to see the establishment of the Center for Economic Education at the University of Tennessee at Chattanooga. This Center can help focus these efforts and provide a link with other efforts to enhance the economic literacy and understanding of our fellow citizens as well as the students who will soon join our ranks.

Experienced-Based Learning

by Marilyn Kourilsky

How can we enhance economic education? Or perhaps more appropriately: How can we enhance the *methodology* of economic education?

For over thirty years professional economic educators have been lamenting the economic illiteracy of the American populace and trying—for the most part unsuccessfully—to find ways of decreasing the gap between what people know and what they should know for effective citizenry. Now even the media are echoing the cry, airing television advertisements that ask, "What's your E.Q. (Economics Quotient)?" and encouraging citizens to send for a booklet which will help them become familiar with their own economic system.

But despite the availability of printed materials explaining basic economic facts and attempts to integrate economics components into standard public school curricula, the people of the United States continue to act in ways which reveal a paucity of economic understanding. This economic ignorance is to the individual's and society's detriment.

The stories of young couples who take second mortgages at annual interest rates of 25 percent, or the consumers in low-income neighborhoods who unknowingly pay 2 to 20 cents more per grocery item than their counterparts in more affluent areas, are too frequent to be simply anecdotal. And the future citizens—three out of every four junior high school students surveyed in thirteen thousand schools by the same council—are no more knowledgeable about economics. They were unable to differentiate, for example, between descriptions of capitalistic and socialistic economies.

Thus it is obvious that generally the school experience does not prepare students for their real-world roles as consumers, job-holders, savers, and investors. Moreover, a lack of familiarity with basic economic principles impairs their effectiveness as citizens sharing in political decisions that impact on us all.

Since a modicum of economics has traditionally been included in social studies classes, it appears that strategic reform should focus on improved teaching of these concepts. Certainly it seems unwise to devote substantial resources to refining the content of curriculum- and teacher-training programs in the schools of education until the actual *methods* of teaching economics are improved. The discussion that follows will present in detail certain such methods, proven successful because the learners themselves become an integral, participatory part of their own education. Other successful methods also exist; but because of my first-hand familiarity with my own methods, I will confine my discussion to them alone.

Unique Reforms Through the Use of Experience-Based Programs in Economics

Reforms in the teaching of economic concepts usually have been presented as units of study, upgraded in economic content, but similar in design and approach (and shortcomings) to the traditional curriculum in their disconnection from a student's daily life. Such refinements will be of little help if the students continue to miss the applicability to their own lives. In contrast, expeience shows that an entirely different type of reform—experience-based learning—can strikingly improve both the students' intellectual grasp of the concepts and their ability to apply them in actual decision-making situations.

I have designed economic education programs to help students learn by doing, to cope better with the realities of the secular world, to discover their entrepreneurial proclivities. These tested and validated programs are designed for kindergarten through twelfth-graders, and for their parents. Youngsters participating in the KEEP (Kourilsky Economic Education Programs) series—Kinder-Economy (grades K–2), Mini-Society (grades 3–6), and Max-Economy I and II (junior and senior high)— have not only surpassed the economic literacy level of a key sample of this country's adult population, but have also demonstrated increases in their self-concept, autonomy, assertiveness, positive attitude toward school and learning, as well as achievement in math and reading.

Parents of children in Mini-Society who have participated in the Co-Learner Parent Education program have increased their own economic literacy level as well as having a positive impact on the economic education of their children. These experience-based programs are modeled on three principles of learning. That learning is enhanced when students participate in:

1. *Personal* as opposed to *vicarious* experiences;
2. *Active* rather than *passive* roles in the learning situation; and
3. *Actual decision-making* in which they will bear the consequences.

Although all the programs share the elements of a concentration on economics and the utilization of an experience-based approach, the K–12 programs were designed for students at specific stages of development and complement existing curriculum at the appropriate school level. To date, the pre-collegiate programs have been implemented in thirty-four states and are enjoying considerable success in terms of demonstrated cognitive and affective results. A brief description of each program, the theoretical basis, and the results of research conducted as follows:

Mini-Society (Grades 3–6) At present the most widely implemented of the KEEP series is Mini-Society, a self-organizing, experience-based approach to teaching economics and other social sciences in grades three through six. In the Mini-Society approach to instruction, students actually experience and then resolve various economic and social problems through the creation and development of their own classroom society. The program is comprised of two interwoven components: the experience itself, and the formal, on-the-spot debriefing of the concepts and ideas derived from the experience.

The Mini-Society works in practice as follows: The system is initiated by a scarcity situation, activated by the teacher, such as "not enough felt-tip pens to go around." Scarcity (limited resources versus relatively unlimited wants) is the central economic problem and impetus for the formation of any economy. Once the children have experienced the scarcity problem, they are assembled into an interaction-discussion group where they inquire into the possible resolutions of the problem and make various other decisions regarding the structure and administration of their small society.

It is in this discussion (debriefing) group that they develop standards of conduct and activities for which they will be paid in the Mini-Society currency. The children are immediately motivated to design and print currency for their society, not unlike "Monopoly" money in appearance, but with real buying power in the Mini-Society. This currency will be used to bid for the scarce resources (such as felt-tip pens) and thereby settle the question of who gets them.

As the society swings into action, the children begin to buy and sell goods and services such as pencils, erasers, and their time. In response to consumer demand, some children develop businesses which range from simple billfold factories to elaborately conceived insurance companies. Other children become salaried workers, rejecting the idea of "going into business for themselves." In conducting the daily business and social activities of the Mini-Society, children are *experiencing* adult life in a microcosm. They experience many of the same problems confronting any economy and are able to explore solutions to both personal and societal economic problems.

In each Mini-Society classroom the children encounter a number of predictable dilemmas which the teachers are specifically trained to debrief. For example, a child starts to produce wallets so other children will have a place to keep their money. Another child sees the high price received by the wallet producer and decides to compete by opening another wallet firm. The price of wallets naturally decreases. The class now assembles under the direction of the teacher in a formal debriefing session on the effects of increased entry (supply) on price. Here the children's actual experience in the classroom society is used for an inquiry lesson, *enhancing* the children's learning and retention of relevant concepts. There are twenty-five such predictable dilemmas which will occur in some variation in most economic systems.

The debriefing sessions cover a whole range of problem situations including economic shortages, inflated currencies, disagreement among partners, whether or not to go into business, whether and when to change employment, economic surpluses and unemployment, sunk costs, whether to hire a friend, unacceptable money, the question of a bank, working versus stealing, charity versus compensation, and why some people are rich and others poor. Thus, Mini-Society is an ongoing process of directly experiencing mature economic, social, ethical, and political problems, exploring various resolutions and their implications, and instituting solutions and experiencing the consequences of one's decisions.

Because the Mini-Society is not just a simulation but a real world to the students, it becomes a highly motivating instructional system, encouraging independent, creative, self-directed inquiry learning by the students, with guidance from the teacher.

Teachers are trained to implement Mini-Society in their classrooms through participation in a workshop of approximately twenty-four contact hours. Workshops are conducted by one or more certified Mini-Society Training Teachers who are experts in the field of economic education. Over 500 workshops have been conducted throughout the United States during the past five years and over 15,000 teachers trained through these workshops are implementing the system in their classrooms.

There are three components to the Mini-Society workshop, covered in an initial twenty to twenty-four hours of training (generally held over two weekends) and, supplementally, in a short follow-up meeting approximately two months later. These components are: "Getting It Started," which covers the philosophical bases of Mini-Society and the formative steps for implementation; "Moving It Ahead," which specifies methods and techniques for judging progress and encouraging business activity; "Enriching Mini-Society and Keeping It Going," in which the teachers are trained to recognize the economic dilemmas arising in the Mini-Society. The teachers then review the issues requiring values clarification and are trained to conduct appropriate debriefing sessions.

Mini-Society recurring economic dilemmas have been encapsulated in case studies, titled in the children's own words:

"We Thought We Could Become Rich Quick"
"But It was My Idea!"
"I've Grown Allergic to My Partner"
"Shortages, Shortages, Shortages (or) Who Gets the Piano Lessons?"
"How Do I Know Anybody Will Buy My Product?"
"The Case of the Unbought Raisins"
"Should I Change My Job?"
"Why Shouldn't I Cry Over Spilled Milk?"
"Should I Hire My Buddy?"
"We Only Accept Quibblings in Poohville"
"Do We Want a Bank?"
"Is it Easier to Steal Than to Work (or) I Hate to Work"
"The Non-Monetary Decision (or) Should We Charge for Everything?"
"Did I Really Make a Profit?"
"Why are Some People Rich and Others Poor?"
"He's Got More Than I Got"
"Copycat, You Dirty Rat"
"The Bunny Plop"
"What Do You Mean You're Broke?"

A number of empirical research studies have revealed the effects of the Mini-Society program. One pilot study including children from fourteen classes indicated that students who had participated in Mini-Society had a significant advantage over those who did not in their understanding of fundamental economic concepts. Another study, using 2,000 children from diverse geographical areas, has upheld these findings, verifying the fact that the high level of economic understanding achieved by Mini-Society participants was not an isolated or one-shot effect. This study also showed that Mini-Society children attained a superior grasp of the roles of consumers and businesses, the function of government in the economy, and the interrelationships among consumers, businesses, banks, and governments.

The research has also revealed some noteworthy aspects of the program's impact on children's psychological well-being. Following participation in a Mini-Society, students have been shown to see themselves as having greater control over their actions than they did prior to the Mini-Society experience. This measure probably is indicative of the degree of autonomy felt by an individual over events in his/her life. The ability, after Mini-Society participation, to be more assertive was also upheld by the research. The same students also exhibited a more positive attitude toward school and learning, and improved self-concepts.

The following anecdote illustrates the enthusiasm engendered by Mini-Society participation. It seems that in a number of classes students enjoyed participation in Mini-Society so much that they came to school despite colds and flu. In one such class, a law was passed penalizing students who attended school with temperatures of more than two degrees over normal. In this same class, one enterprising entrepreneur began offering health insurance and did a booming business.

Much of the research data has also pointed to the fact that many children held stereotyped images of people in entrepreneurial roles. We found that children between the ages of 8 and 12 tended to greatly overestimate the percentage of profit realized on the investment of the average American entrepreneur. Children also depicted entrepreneurs in an extremely stereotypical manner. Many drawings showed corpulent, balding men, sweating profusely and chewing hungrily on large cigars. Captions often indicated that students considered profits too large and the dealings of businesspeople dishonest.

Following participation in Mini-Society, students exhibited a more realistic understanding of the percentage of profits enjoyed by the average entrepreneur (a situation which may arise from their own Mini-Society entrepreneurial experiences). They also depicted businesspeople in a much less stereotyped manner. Entrepreneurs drawn were of both sexes and their physical appearances varied to the same degree that children's drawings of people in general vary. Perhaps most significant was the fact that the drawings frequently resembled the students themselves.

Also in the psychological domain was the students' manifestation of a greater willingness to take risks following participation in the program. This suggests that their own experiences as entrepreneurs in Mini-Society may have altered their attitude toward actions which they previously considered too venturesome. Since moderate risk-taking is one of the characteristics necessary for the success of any business venture we considered this a positive finding.

We have studied recent data in an attempt to determine what predictors of entrepreneurship might be evidenced in elementary school age children. We found that there are distinct sex differences with reference to both the initiation of an entrepreneurial venture and subsequent entrepreneurial success. For boys, persistence, actual success in business, and understanding of economic concepts most strongly identified those who became successful entrepreneurs.

These same three characteristics also were strong predictors of success in girl entrepreneurs; however, a perception of themselves as successful was the *most* powerful predictor for girls' success, followed by persistence, "field independence," and economic understanding. These findings suggest that it may be necessary to nurture slightly different characteristics in boys and girls in order to achieve equitable preparation for certain economic roles.

Kinder-Economy (Grades K–2) Most educators believe that economics is a subject suitable only for high school or college study, but the results of our pilot studies at the K–2 grade level indicate that children as young as five who participate in a Kinder-Economy program can identify and comprehend scarcity, supply, demand, opportunity cost, and other related concepts. In addition, young children can apply these concepts to the situations within their own frame of reference.

The Kinder-Economy is a set of sequential experiences that emphasizes decision-making concepts of economics related to the real world. The program is designed to be implemented for thirty minutes a day throughout a semester. Like the Mini-Society, the Kinder-Economy is predicated on the educational philosophy of experience-based instruction. In the case of Kinder-Economy, however, the children do *not* create a society but instead participate in seven experience-based simulations.[1]

---

[1] Children participating in a simulation are aware that they are role-playing and think of their situation as a "pretend" experience as opposed to the core of their reality.

With the Kinder-Economy, the children first experience and live with the repercussions of the concept to be emphasized. For example, children may be exposed to a number of scarcity situations drawn from the classroom until each child is able to recognize and identify as "scarcity" what he or she is experiencing. The teacher then debriefs the children about the scarcity situations and helps them to identify the concept they have experienced and suggest possible solutions to the problems they have encountered.

The teacher now *reinforces* the experiences through games, learning centers, worksheets, and sometimes filmstrips (e.g., a concentration-type matching game may be developed in which the children identify scarcity situations). Because of the differences in learning styles and rates, we find that it is in stage three that the concept is "cemented" in the minds of the children.

A concept such as opportunity cost is introduced as children identify alternatives involved in decisions they make in school, such as which of two activities to participate in (the monkey bars or jump rope) or which supplies to use to create something. The children use cost-benefit analysis in considering whether they have made a "good" decision.

In the upper elementary school, children as Mini-Society citizens consider their classrooms—as opposed to the outside world—to be their society. In the Kinder-Economy, children are too young and too egocentric to perceive themselves as part of a society. To a K–2 grade child, the society is the individual, and the individual sees each experience largely as unique to himself or herself.

The results of our research on the effectiveness of the Kinder-Economy students' understanding of economic concepts was substantially higher than non-Kinder-Economy children. In fact, the Kinder-Economy "graduate" almost always possesses greater economic savvy than the average adult in our society.

Max-Economy I (Junior High/Middle School) and Max-Economy II (Senior High) The Max-Economy programs require the involvement and team work of several teachers from the same secondary school. In a school with traditional departmentalization, this would generally include at least one teacher from either social studies or business and at least one teacher from vocational arts and/or home economics.

Students in Max-Economy programs participate in a modified market economy in which they are free to use their own resources (such as time and energy) in an activity of their choice. Similarly, they may choose *not* to use their resources to participate in the economy. In a market economy the individual makes choices as to how to utilize his/her resources based largely on personal judgments. It is through this decision-making and sometimes risk-taking process that students learn to apply economics and business concepts as well as verbal persuasion and manual skills to the real world. (Such application is enhanced if students have access to a Junior Achievement facility in the neighborhood.)

After the necessary grounding in economic and business concepts and methods, the students are given an opportunity to apply their knowledge in the development of a business. In this way, Max-Economy students are given a preview of the adult world of business. While their successes are applauded, they are also carefully analyzed. So, too, are their mistakes; and the opportunity to "blow it" in a relatively safe environment is a significant aspect of the Max-Economy experience. Both successes and failures are discussed and used as a springboard for further learning and the application of new ideas.

Co-Learner Parent Education The Co-Learner Parent Education Program generally begins with the children of the parent-learners participating in a classroom Mini-Society (although in some cases, depending on the children's grade level, participation may be in some form of simulated economy rather than Mini-Society). The economic dilemmas faced by the Mini-Societies, specifically those societies in which the children of the parent-learners are participating, are collected and transformed into case studies.

These dilemmas have application both to economics and values-clarification. The parents, in biweekly adult-tutorial seminars, then study and attempt to resolve these dilemmas experienced by their children. An economic education evaluates the reasoning powers and economic knowledge of the parents, who are taught economics on a case-by-case "need to know" basis. After the parents have outlined and substantiated their solutions to the case studies, the children who experienced the dilemmas are invited to the adult seminars to explain the actual ways in which they resolved the specific dilemmas in question. Often a child must actually teach the parent an economic concept to effectively support the alternatives he chose.

After both the parents and children have demonstrated skill in economic analysis with regard to Mini-Society dilemmas, they are asked to apply economic reasoning in resolving hypothetical family dilemmas such as whether to buy a pet, whether to go to summer camp or summer school, or even whether the family should buy a new car.

The results of the pilot study of the Co-Learner approach to Parent Education revealed that the participating parents' economic understanding sharply increased. It also showed that the children of these parents showed greater increases in learning than the norm, suggesting that there are positive consequences resulting from parental encouragement and the sharing of instructional activities. This instruction also tended to bring about changes in the attitudes of both the parents and children toward business, especially with respect to their image of the entrepreneur.

It is important to note that improvement in economic understanding of students as well as parents was extraordinary, suggesting that economic illiteracy can be alleviated if economic education and awareness become important priorities in our society and in our schools.

In a follow-up study of the co-learner approach, it was also found that parents and children could be taught to use cost-benefit analysis in their daily joint decisions, and that the use of such economic reasoning increased satisfaction with their decision-making process.

The Use of Imposed Behavior Modification

All too frequently experience-based economic education involves the instructor's *imposing* behavioral changes rather than exposing the students to the ideas and possibilities of change that would occur through the students' own actions. In a true experience-based learning situation the teacher assists the students in identifying the problem, analyzing its components and exploring the alternative solutions.

A case in point is the well-intentioned but misguided teacher who rewarded those students who "cleaned their plates" at lunch. One enterprising young man, with an epicurean bent, saw an opportunity which he quickly seized. He approached his classmates with the offer of cleaning their plates for a price. This willing and astute entrepreneur even evidenced his grasp of pricing practices by charging more to consume leftover spinach than to finish another child's jello salad. Needless to say, this boy's parents were more concerned with his increasing bulk than his entrepreneurial creativity.

Adherence to the philosophy of experience-based education demands that instructors *expose* students to stimuli which may change behavior rather than impose specific behavioral changes. While there is little doubt that imposed behavior modification may prove successful in some instances, it definitely has less successful results when compared with an experience-based economic education program in such terms as economic knowledge, autonomy, and assertiveness. Students' frequent reaction to imposed behavior modification is production decreases in the work situation. One reason for the decrease is that students who lack feelings of autonomy can see little reason to exert effort in entrepreneurial roles.

The Misuse of Economics

A second abuse of experience-based economic education centers on the misuse or misunderstanding of economic concepts. The cause of economic literacy certainly is not assisted by instructors teaching incorrect economics. An example of one such disservice to students and society-at-large was observed in a classroom where diverse businesses were being established and consumer sovereignty dictated the emergence of a bank. Seeing the success enjoyed by the owners of the fledgling bank, two children decided to form a partnership to provide competing banking services. They were halted by the teacher who indicated that the society already had a bank and that they must create another business idea. The creation of monopolies by an uninformed teacher is not the sole infraction of this type.

Another teacher was agitated when his children, unbeknown to him, derived the concept of interest. A child wanted to charge another child a price for borrowing money. Unaware that the children had discovered the concept of interest (the price of money) the teacher explained to them that charging for the use of money was exploitative and unethical. In a third instance, a private postal service had driven the government-owned postal service out of business by charging lower rates and delivering mail among classrooms more efficiently. The teacher announced that post offices *had* to be run by government because "that's the way it's done."

Most of the teachers who incorrectly implement have not been trained formally, they are usually imitating incorrectly the teacher next door. However, there are other teachers who have been trained and still abort the goals of the systems. In the name of Mini-Society, Kinder-Economy, or Max-Economy, they actually believed they were establishing "desirable" modifications or extensions.

All of the tactics described above resulted in some type of learning. However, such modifications violate the conceptual framework of experience-based economic education as well as mutilate the effective implementation of instructional systems designed to increase and improve autonomy, self-concept, and attitudes toward learning.

Conclusion

In the last decade the educational sector has been inundated with so many advances in technology that it has become more than a little tempting to put the children in front of the tube, be it TV, video-cassettes, filmstrips, etc., and watch them passively glean information.

On the other hand, enough literature on the advantages of actively participating in the learning process and the importance of the affective domain have motivated the teacher to seek out instructional strategies that go beyond "talking at the children." Regardless of the quality of the delivery, be it the great Cicero or the bumbling Zeke, children spend, in addition to an average of five hours a day in front of the TV at home, another several hours in passive learning situations in the classroom.

It has been the purpose of this article to provide an alternative (and not just for children) to the "sit on your derriere" approach to learning. The conceptual basis for, as well as a detailed amplification of, several experience-based models of instruction have been described.

One can conjecture—and the success of the programs certainly appears to corroborate—that experience-based programs such as those described result in dramatic increases in learning, both cognitively and affectively. What are the reasons for these outcomes? Do they apply only to disciplines such as economics?

First, consider the highly emotional tone and degree of personal involvement inherent in experience-based instructional programs. The learner is *part* of the action, not an observer. The recall is of an experience that actually happened.

Secondly, the debriefing, if correctly implemented, capsulizes, focuses, and extends the learning experience. It is not just the experience that creates the learning; an integral part of experience-based instruction is the quality of the debriefing.

For a debriefing to be optimal it is necessary for the following to occur:
1. The learner verbally describes the experience.
2. A problem related to the experience is isolated.
3. The learners are provided with the tools to analyze the problem.
4. Tentative solutions are discussed and analyzed.
5. The bottom-line consequences to the individual and to society are verbalized and discussed.

Remember, however, it is imperative that the teacher have something concrete and viscerally encompassing to debrief.

Third, the individual who had the experience and participated in an inquiry-oriented debriefing may now have to make a decision as a result of the experience. This third dimension of learning—personally bearing the bottom-line consequences of one's decision—is also an integral part of the experience-based models of education presented in this paper. Note that the latter was an *essential* characteristic of all the programs described. An individual may learn from pretending (s)he is an Eskimo and deciding what to do under given hypothetical conditions. However, our research seems to suggest that an individual may gain considerably more when making that decision for himself/herself and then bearing the bottom-line consequences.

Although the instructional systems described in this article relate more to values-clarification and economics/social science than to other disciplines, it is highly probable that the learning principles exposited can be extended to other areas of study.

Hopefully we will improve economic literacy by offering experience-based (not just activities-oriented) education as an option to totally didactic instruction. Eventually the extension of such an approach may also improve the literacy in other disciplines.

Bibliography

Hereford, Carl F. *Changing Parental Attitudes through Group Discussion.* Austin: Univ. of Texas Press, 1963.

Karnes, Merle, et al. "The Impact of At-Home Instruction by Mothers on Performance in the Ameliorative Pre-School." *In Research and Development Program on Pre-school Disadvantaged Children. Final Report.* Urbana: Univ. of Illinois, Institute of Research for Exceptional Children, May 1969, pp. 205–12.

Kourilsky, Marilyn. *Beyond Simulation: The Mini-Society Approach to Instruction in Economics and Other Social Sciences.* Los Angeles: Educational Resource Associates, 1974.

Kourilsky, Marilyn. "A Co-Learner Approach to Parent/Child Economic Education: An Empirical Investigation." Appendix F in *The Extension, Longitudinal Evaluation and Leadership Replication of the Mini-Society and Kinder-Economy Learning Systems. Final Report.* Prepared for the Board of Directors, Charles Stewart Mott Foundation, Flint, Mich., 1978.

Kourilsky, Marilyn. *The Extension, Longitudinal Evaluation and Leadership Replication of the Mini-Society and Kinder-Economy Learning Systems. Final Report.* Prepared for the Board of Directors, Charles Stewart Mott Foundation, Flint, Mich., 1978.

Kourilsky, Marilyn. *The Implementation of Experienced-Based Learning Systems in California, Utah and Colorado: A Cooperative Program in Economic Education. Final Report.* Prepared for Standard Oil Company of California, San Francisco, June 1977.

Kourilsky, Marilyn. "The Kinder-Economy: A Case Study of Kindergarten Pupils' Acquisition of Economic Concept." *The Elementary School Journal*, Jan. 1977, pp. 77, 182–91.

Kourilsky, Marilyn. "Optimal Intervention: An Empirical Investigation of the Role of the Teacher in Experience-Based Instruction." *Journal of Experimental Education*, in press.

Kourilsky, Marilyn. "Perceived Versus Actual Risk-Taking in Mini-Societies." *Social Studies*, Sept./Oct. 1976, pp. 67, 191–94.

Kourilsky, Marilyn. "Predictors of Entrepreneurship in a Simulated Economy." Appendix A in *The Extension, Longitudinal Evaluation and Leadership Replication of the Mini-Society and Kinder-Economy Learning Systems. First Interim Report, Year II*. Prepared for the Board of Directors, Charles Stewart Mott Foundation, Flint, Mich., 1979.

Kourilsky, Marilyn & Hirshleifer, Jack. "Mini-Society vs. Token Economy: An Experimental Comparison of the Effects on Learning and Autonomy of Socially Emergent and Imposed Behavior Modification." *Journal of Educational Research*, July/ Aug. 1976, pp. 69, 376–81.

Maccoby, Eleanor Emmons. (Ed.), *The Development of Sex Differences*. Stanford: Stanford Univ. Press, 1966.

Mancuso, Joseph R. *How to Start, Finance and Manage Your Own Small Business*. Englewood Cliffs, N.J.: Prentice-Hall, 1978.

Piaget, Jean & Barbel, I. *The Psychology of the Child*. New York: Basic Books, 1969.

Radin, Norma. "Three Degrees of Maternal Involvement in a Preschool Program: Impact on Mothers and Children." *Child Development*, Dec. 1972, pp. 43, 135–64.

IV

Who Is Responsible for Economic Education—Parents, Teachers or the Public School System?

by Mary Ellen Oliverio

A group of successful high school juniors and seniors were participants in an international meeting of youth in Europe one summer not too long ago. In the informal encounters outside the scheduled meetings, the youth began to talk among themselves. Inevitably, there were questions about their respective countries. The American youth were stunned when they were asked:

What makes your economy so prosperous?
Why isn't every person in the United States guaranteed a job?
What does your Government do when it thinks the citizens are spending too much money?

The adults who served as chaperones said that the American youth came to them seeking information to aid them in answering questions. The adults tried to be helpful. One chaperone, after his return to the States, stated:

The experience was an amazing one on several counts. The American students were asked questions that they had never even *thought* about concerning their society. Our students realized that they knew little; they saw how much more the student leaders from other countries seem to know about their economies. We adults realized that here, too, was another area where possibly there were weaknesses in the public school curriculum. We began to wonder what was the general knowledge of economics among high school students generally if this so-called leadership group knew so little. We began to wonder who's responsible for providing this kind of education.

This is our task: to consider who is indeed responsible for

economic education. I have taken the point of view that there is shared responsibility for all of education—including economic education—in the American society. While the responsibility of the school system differs from that of the teacher and from that of the parents, there are common as well as unique considerations worthy of our attention. Our purpose is simple: to optimize the level of economic understanding in the society. The question is: How?

The Responsibility of the Public School System

Leadership for the program of the public schools is actually a shared responsibility. The boards of education of the several states design the general purposes for the schools; local school boards, directors of curriculum, and principals establish more specific goals for school programs. Additionally, the leadership of large professional education organizations influence the direction and goals of the school.

We cannot talk about the responsibility for economic education at the state and local level without first recognizing the present status of leadership in education. As illustrative of the present situation, we have only to note the topics in professional journals such as *Educational Leadership* or *NASSP Bulletin* (National Association of Secondary School Principals). To a considerable extent, the articles reflect reactions to the pressures felt in the educational establishment.

When a public relations executive of one of the largest professional education groups in the United States was asked: "What do you state as the general purposes of the school in the present era?," the executive responded: "How do you expect us to have a general statement? Don't you realize that the schools face pressures from all sides? The schools can hardly react to the pressures. We could never write a statement that would satisfy all the groups that are putting pressure on us." It appears that in state after state special interest groups with well-organized strategies are having success in getting their wishes. The educational leadership is seemingly unable to establish priorities and make judgments independently of these outside pressures.

Our purpose is not to comprehend educational leadership in our schools, so there is no time to talk about the matter in depth.

The topic is pertinent to us in a general way, because we care about the judgments to be made concerning economic education.

We can assume an optimistic position and trust that the educational establishment will move toward a synthesis of the varying demands made and will establish a clear statement of the social responsibility of the schools in our society. We will hope that the state boards will return to the question: What is the unique responsibility of the school in our society? And I would hope at such a time that our educational leadership will reassess the time-honored three-fold public school responsibility that has been stated again and again in simple terms:

- The schools have a responsibility to transmit the cultural heritage of our world...
- The schools have a responsibility to develop the critical thinking of students...
- The schools have a responsibility to develop intellectual skills.

Those of us who think that economic education is an important component of public education are convinced that careful attention to specifying the school program relative to the three responsibilities of the school will lead to appropriate inclusion of economic understandings throughout the school program.

We would say that it is the public school's task to determine the framework within which economic education is organized. The educational leadership at the state and local levels must give attention to these questions:
1. What theoretical structure of the field of economics should be introduced to students in the public schools?
2. What level of understanding of the structure should students have to be able to intelligently read and discuss contemporary topics and to be able to continue to learn about the field?
3. What economic history should students know as a basis for understanding the contemporary world and for assessing predictions and general notions about the future?
4. What are the personal and business economic skills that students should develop under the auspices of the school?

We cannot conclude this brief discussion of the responsibility of the total school without recognizing the extent to which the educational leadership has considered economics as a part of the school program. In 1940 Erling M. Hunt in a review of what the schools had attempted in economic education commented:

> Formal economics courses have been offered in some American secondary schools for nearly 120 years. The subject has, however, occupied an unimportant and uninfluential position, usually as a half-year course in the last year of high school, unavailable to the large number who left school early, and not elected by many of those who have remained.[1]

Earlier in the same article, which was a presentation at a conference on education and economic literacy, Hunt stated:

> Economic competence has not been a major concern of American education as a whole in the past. It rarely is so now. Most schools did not even offer economics until well into the twentieth century. Some still do not offer it, and in those that do it is frequently an elective which many students ignore. Often, moreover, the kind of economics offered has little to do with economic competence.[2]

Hunt was reviewing the situation as of late 1939. In the next decade, the Joint Council on Economic Education was established as a permanent organization to coordinate and encourage continuing work to improve economic education throughout the school system in the United States.[3] In 1960 the Committee for Economic Development and the American Economic Association created a National Task Force on Economic Education that had as its mission to describe the minimum understanding of economics essential for good citizenship and attainable by high school students.[4] The Task Force report, issued in September 1961, stimulated considerable activity in the field of economic

---

[1] Erling M. Hunt, "Developing Economic Competence Through Public Education," *Teachers College Record*, April 1940, p. 574.
[2] *Ibid.*
[3] Joint Council on Economic Education, *Annual Report for Fiscal Year Ended June 30, 1978*.
[4] The National Task Force on Economic Education, *Economic Education in the Schools, A Summary*, Committee for Economic Development, Sept. 1961, p. 4.

education. Yet in the late '70's the statistics still do not reflect a high level of concern:
- It is estimated that less than 3 percent of the country's entire high school population take a course in economics.
- Only 13 states require economics for high school students.
- Only slightly more than one-fourth of the secondary schools in the United States offer a course in economics.
- Only seven states require a K-12 economic education program.[5]

A serious study needs to be done on why economic education has not been able to gain a foothold in our school systems. Later, I shall discuss a few barriers to the implementation of programs in economic education.

The Responsibility of Teachers

Teacher implement the goals established by the school system. In this role they are translators of often abstract aims, such as "to develop an understanding of the socio-economic world in which students live." It is the teachers who must design and redesign what is to be provided in the classroom. I don't mean to imply that there is no interaction between the administrators and the teachers. There are, of course, many situations when common concerns are cooperatively studied and evaluated. However, here we shall spotlight what the teacher must accept as primary responsibilities.

First, the teachers must be forever aware of the shifting considerations for which the school is accepting responsibility or should accept responsibility. For example, the alert teacher contemplates the impact of a statement such as that made by Robert J. Havighurst recently as he considered the curriculum for a post-industrial society. Havighurst stated:

> Out of the present perplexity and complexity of the curriculum, and looking ahead to the nature of the post-industrial society, we may state three basic propositions:

---

[5]Excerpted from a brochure prepared by the Joint Council on Economic Education, 1979. (As of late 1981, 29 states now require high school economics.)

1. The curriculum should stress the structure of the subjects that are studied, rather than the student storing up discrete bits of information.
2. The curriculum should support a constructive and democratic pluralism. This will contribute to:
   a. Mutual appreciation and understanding of every subculture by the other ones.
   b. Freedom for each subculture to practice its culture and socialize its children.
   c. Sharing by each group in the economic and civic life of the society.
   d. Peaceful coexistence of diverse life styles, folkways, manners, language patterns, religious beliefs and practices, and family structures.
3. The curriculum should convey to all youth a body of shared knowledge and experience that helps them to grow up and live successfully in the post-industrial society. This applies especially to the area of the social sciences, with the middle school and the high school teaching what is appropriate about the following topics:

Technology of post-industrial society, including energy policy and problems
Population problems
The civics and economics of metropolitan areas, including renewal of the central city
Monetary problems and issues—inflation
World interdependency of nations[6]

The sensitive teacher reads such statements and carefully assesses the value of each item. For those items that seem wise, the teacher begins a process of reviewing what he (she) does with an open mind, striving to see if alternative content or alternative instructional method should be substituted for what is presently done. The effective teacher has the responsibility for checking out the relevant goals and emerging demands made by new statements of purpose.

Second, the teacher must keep informed of what is happening in the field of economics and related areas. The effective teacher is forever a scholar. Those teachers who have a responsibility for teaching economic understanding must appreciate the evolutionary nature of the field. A teacher who studied formal eco-

---

[6]Robert J. Havighurst, "Common Experience Versus Diversity in the Curriculum," *Educational Leadership*, Nov. 1978, pp. 120–21.

nomics fifteen or twenty years ago and has given no further attention to the subject matter will surely be out of date. The teacher must design a way of continuing to study. Since teachers are technicians in learning theory, they should be able to determine an effective learning program for themselves. Through independent study, through organized instruction in university or college, through study groups informally organized, the teacher can remain a dynamic learner of his (her) subject field.

Third, the teacher must be able to critically evaluate the materials that are available. The teacher should be able to identify the omissions, the biases, the points of view in books, films, filmstrips, pamphlets, articles, and similar materials that may be used for instructional purposes. Critical evaluation is necessary for two purposes: The teacher must determine if the material is appropriate for use in instruction, and the teacher must determine the manner in which the material will be used. Let me attempt to illustrate what I mean.

The teacher reads an article entitled "The Free Enterprise System: Essential for American Survival." The writer states several times that the teacher must be a "partner in the vital economic education movement" and that the teacher will be such a partner if he (she) teaches the truth about economics. Throughout the article there are implications that the free enterprise system and the contemporary business society are identical. The author is, in effect, saying that the competitive market economy is equivalent to the present system of business.

The teacher must ask: "What is missing here?" "What is this author trying to tell me?" On careful reading, the teacher recognizes that the businessman/author is attempting to establish that the pure competitive model from classical economics is the reality of modern American economic life. What does the teacher learn from such an article? The teacher learns that his (her) students must indeed understand the theoretical notions about economics behavior, but they must also understand the nature in which economic behavior in the market place differs from the classical mode. The author, the teacher will note, doesn't provide operational definitions for "free enterprise" or "free choice." The author is trying to persuade the teacher; his approach is that of a polemist, not that of an instructor. Yet, the insightful teacher learns much from such a writing.

Let's look at another illustration. The teacher gets a bulletin provided by a nonprofit group that is interested in aiding the teacher as he (she) plans for the development of economic competencies in the elementary school. Under the heading, "Goods and services are sold at a profit," the teacher reads:

> It costs money to manufacture a car, bake a loaf of bread, bottle a quart of milk, or make a dress. When the producer sells an article, therefore, he charges enough so that he covers his cost and also so that he makes a profit. If he did not make a profit, he would soon be out of business. All of his workers would then become unemployed. The manufacturer needs to make a profit in order to have funds: (1) to replace worn-out tools; (2) to provide for expansion and growth; (3) to create a reserve fund to take care of emergency breakdowns; and (4) to maintain a good financial record. Girls sell Girl Scout Cookies for more than what the troop paid for them. The difference between what the troop receives (income) and what the troop paid (cost) is called earnings (profit). The profit helps to make the program (selling the cookies) worthwhile.

Let us hope that the teacher knows how the accountant determines profit as well as what the economic concept of profit is. If the teacher's knowledge comes from this excerpt, the students will fail to get the essence of the extremely fascinating concept of profit.

Fourth, the teacher must understand what students seek in their learning. Teachers should not underestimate the intellectual yearnings of students. As an illustration of this point, I would like to share with you some findings from a very informal survey that an exceptional teacher in a metropolitan New York high school undertook. In a brief questionnaire, the students were asked this question:

> At this time, February 1979, what do you believe you should know about economics and the condition of our country in relation to other countries that you do not know?

Forty-two juniors and seniors responded to this question. While the responses varied, not *one* student identified a person-

al economic matter such as learning how to buy wisely or how to save money. Answers were like these:
- I would like to know the extent to which the U.S. is dependent on other countries.
- I would like to know more about the major world powers and how their economies compare with ours.
- I would be interested in the comparison of the various economic systems in the world.
- I would like to understand more about recessions and prosperity.

In a college course in economics, several students commented that while they had had an economics course in high school, they hadn't learned any economics. As one student stated:

The teacher thought we wanted "fun and games" so we pretended we were buyers of stock and managers of business. It was all a lot of busy work. We never did any *thinking* about economic topics.

I realize the foregoing are anecdotal comments and I don't want to imply that generalizations are appropriate. It is interesting to note, though, that in the most recent issues of *Economic Education Experiences of Enterprising Teachers*, a publication that describes the best entries submitted in the National Awards Program for Excellence in Teaching Economics, there was not one experience described that involved an international aspect of economics. Many of the best experiences would have been assessed by the college students in the economic class to which I briefly referred as trivial and dealing with that which was not of most consequence.

Fifth, the teacher must skillfully assess the alternative ways of providing instruction. How are basic concepts to be developed? How can students learn to deal with controversial issues? How can students be introduced to the task of assessing alternative decision, and evaluating the quality of decisions? Throughout the consideration of methodology, the teacher must be aware of what his (her) role will be and what the students' role will be. The teacher must remember that there are processes to be developed. The task of the teacher in economic instruction is *not* to present a particular position but rather to instruct students so that they understand how to evaluate information, how to recognize if there is missing information, how to resolve problems and come to conclusions. The student needs to be able to distinguish fact from value, description from analysis, first approximation from detailed revelation. The teacher, as a teacher, has no opinion about the relative value of policy recommendations. Of course, as students develop sophistication in the handling of economic topics and in recognizing the role of opinion, they can be introduced to a teacher's opinion and experience the assessment of such opinion.

Sixth, the teachers must engage in cooperative efforts among themselves in order to maximize the richness of learning experiences. Society is an indivisible whole. We expect students to understand "society." Yet, typically, students study "society" segment by segment—first, looking at it historically, then sociologically, then economically. There are likely to be possibilities for interdisciplinary studies, particularly at the secondary school level that go virtually unexplored in many schools. Teachers tend to work independently. Yet, the explosion of knowledge with the companion development of interrelationships among fields calls for cooperative efforts.

I wonder if our secondary school students would have better insight into their society if they were introduced to fields of knowledge, such as economics, sociology and political science, through a study of problems that cut across such disciplines. Would students learn more if three teachers—an economist, a political scientist, and a sociologist—taught a course entitled "Problems of Democracy" or "Contemporary Problems"? During the course the students would listen to presentations from the three specialists addressing themselves to the same problem, let us say, unemployment, as an example. The three teachers would make their presentations in the presence of each other, so that they could discuss among themselves, for the benefit of the students, points of mutual concern and of controversy.

In addition to listening to the multi-discipline presentation, students would have a chance to study intensively with each of the teachers in relation to at least one problem. So by the end of the course, students would have had the opportunity to see contemporary problems from the point of view of several specialists, and perhaps their view of society be both more realistic and more scholarly.

As we review the extent to which teachers have assumed responsibility for economic education, we don't find a very encouraging state of affairs. We find, for example, that more than 50 percent of social studies teachers have not even had a course in economics. Richard E. Gross in his survey of the status of social studies noted that 56 percent of the teachers had never heard of the special program, Econ 12. He reported that in informal surveys in California and Montana more than 70 percent of the K-12 teachers were doing little or nothing with social studies.[7]

In the questionnaire survey done in a metropolitan New York high school, to which I just referred, only 6 of the 42 respondents could recall any experience from their elementary school days that was related to economic education.

In a survey of high school students who had been elected to *Who's Who Among American High School Students,* the respondents were asked if their high schools had prepared them to understand economics and the American free enterprise system. Sixty-three percent responded that their schools had not fully prepared them in this area.[8]

Shaver, Davis, and Helburn attempted to assess the status of social studies education by reviewing three comprehensive National Science Foundation Studies. Some of their conclusions have relevance for the teaching of economics. Among these are:

> ... The curriculum is mostly history and government, with geography included at the elementary and middle/junior high levels. There is little interdisciplinary teaching, and little attention to societal issues.
>
> ... The dominant modes of instruction continue to be large group, teacher-controlled recitation and lecture, based primarily on the textbook.
>
> ... The "knowing" expected of students is largely information-oriented. ... Students typically are not encouraged to develop systematic modes of inquiry and reasoning.

[7]Richard E. Gross, "The Status of the Social Studies in the Public Schools of the U.S.: Facts and Impressions of a National Survey," *Social Education,* March 1977, p. 196.

[8]Eighth Annual Survey, *Who's Who Among American High School Students,* 1977.

They are expected to learn and respect understandings that come from others.[9]

In developing more effective teaching of economics, there is need for improving the skills of teachers as well as increasing their knowledge of the field. The new Center for Economic Education at the University of Tennessee at Chattanooga has many opportunities to make significant efforts in this field.

The Role of Parents

In general, it seems to me, parents have a responsibility to provide concern and encouragement to their children as they study. At the same time, parents should grant children freedom to be students on their own. Parents must be sensitive to the child's needs and constantly refine their interaction to optimize the child's own development. The task is subtle; it cannot be described easily. We know it is being performed successfully when the child has a sense that as a student he is pursuing "his own destiny," yet at the same time he feels the emotional support of his parents.

The extent to which parents become teacher aides will depend on their knowledge of the particular subjects being studied. In some instances the parent can serve as one more resource as a student strives to comprehend a new concept, grasp a new principle, or work out a new project. In the area of economic understanding, I would see the parents doing nothing more or less than they would do for any other subject being studied.

There is, however, another dimension to economic education: there is the dimension of attitudes and values. Parents are a powerful influence in providing this type of education. The schools seem to have great difficulty in teaching moral values. If parents brought intellectual insight to their own ethical and moral behavior and thereafter improved the level of their behavior, we would have another source of assistance in improving the quality of American life. It is likely that all adults by

---

[9]James P. Shaver, O. L. Davis, Jr., and Suzanne W. Helburn, "The Status of Social Studies Education: Impressions from Three NSF Studies," *Social Education*, Feb. 1979, p. 159.

behavior and not by words are influential citizens.

Let me attempt to illustrate by sharing two comments made by high school students:

A high school senior in a prosperous suburban community was talking with a visiting teacher about his own life and that of his parents. In the course of the conversation he said:

My family is rich, if you mean that the annual income is high. My father is a corporation executive; he has been successful, since he began as a trainee right after college and, as he says, his promotions came fast. But do you know what he is *always* saying: "In ten years I can retire and play golf every day. I can get out of this rat race..." I've been hearing comments like this since I was a kid. I am sick and tired of it. I've asked my Dad, "Why do you stay?" He says: "I want to give my family the good life."

The second comment is from a girl who is a junior in a city high school. She was out of class for three days in early December and when she returned the teacher asked if illness had kept her at home. She replied:

"No, I wasn't sick. I really was sorry to miss class. But, you see, my mother felt she had to take her sick days before the end of the year since she would lose them. In her company you can't accumulate sick days, so my Mother said she and all the others figure out a way near the end of the year to get a little extra vacation. So, she wanted to visit her sister and she made me go with her."

What kind of economic values are these parents presenting to their children? Do they realize what their behavior indicates? Do they know how confusing it is to our youth, for example, to be told we have economic freedom in the American economy but then to have those youth in homes where no one seems to feel that freedom?

When public education was getting underway in the United States, public orators spent much time talking about the quality of human behavior that would result from universal public education. And, as we look at the figures, we realize we have come a long way, as far as providing universal education is concerned. For example, in 1910 the median level of education in the United States was 8.1 years; in 1950 it was 9.3 years; and by 1975 it had reached 12.3 years. This means that today's youth in our elementary and secondary schools have in most instances parents who have had a secondary school education.

The educators of a hundred years ago would have predicted that by this date we would have a level of moral behavior in our country that would make obsolete prisons, correctional institutions, systems for detection of dishonesty, etc. Of course, we realize that these early educators were projecting the effects of education in a far too optimistic light. Yet, are we being naïve— and unduly optimistic—if we think that the quality of ethical behavior vis-a-vis economic behavior is not improvable? I would like to think that it is, especially if parents teach their children moral values.

Here we have another virtually unexplored field in economics: the field of morality about economic behavior and how the level of morality might be raised. I must leave this topic with nothing more revealing to say. I only know there is much to learn.

Barriers to the Implementation of Responsibility

We might well raise the question: Why hasn't there been more acceptance of economic understanding as a component of the education of all youth? There are many reasons for the present state of affairs.

The Persistence of Traditional Subject Matter

Economics is a young discipline. When this country was founded, economics was in its infancy. William Petty, who has been credited with being our first economic analyst, had published his *Treatise of Taxes and Contributions* about a hundred years earlier, in 1662. Adam Smith's *An Inquiry into the Nature and Causes of the Wealth of Nations*, appeared in 1776. Given the slow dissemination of knowledge, the early statements on public education in the United States didn't identify economics as a separate field of study. Some writers and thinkers about education did see the need for a study of commerce by those young men who were going to be merchants. But the study of commerce was a practical, descriptive type of field, they believed; it was in effect a type of applied economics.

As mentioned earlier, economics did begin to appear as a separate subject about 1820, and by the early years of this century there was a considerable amount of applied economics being offered in courses in home economics, business education, and consumer education. However these courses were often intended for students who were not continuing their education. The application of the learning to jobs and to practical life demands was the motivation for the subject matter selected.

Keeping the Course Content Current and Relevant

In the teaching of technical knowledge and skills there is always the problem of obsolescence. This realization has led to the development of a network of continuing education programs for physicians, accountants, electrical engineers, automobile mechanics, internal revenue agents, teachers and school administrators.

But it would appear that more attention is paid to the methodology of instruction than with the actual course content. I have not seen a recent publication from the educational establishment that strives to specify the subject matter and the experiences that are most relevant for the contemporary world.

The earlier quotation from the review done by James P. Shaver and his colleagues reflects a rather static system in the schools, a system without feedback. One comment may illustrate the failure to maintain relevance. In New York State where the Board of Regents is developing a state competency examination, no competence, as measured by a test, has been identified in the areas dealing with civics and citizenship. Has there not been sufficient observations, systematically recorded and assessed, that would form the basis of some measure of competency in this area?

Timidity in Handling Controversial Subject Matter

Economics is perceived by many to be political economics and to be value-laden. Instruction is assumed to be ideological and, therefore, to have no place in the school's program. Further, economics doesn't seem to have any "right" answers and is not, therefore, a useful subject for the school's curriculum.

When we recognize that the schools haven't been effective in designing ways of developing critical thinking ability, we can understand why the ways of thinking about economic phenomena through understanding economic analysis have not made inroads into our public schools.

The Failure of Business to Make Meaningful Contributions

To my knowledge, there has been little explicit specification by school leaders of the potentially most valuable assistance the business community can provide to those who want to develop economic understanding among American elementary and secondary school students.

Business tries to remain aware of its public image. When a public opinion poll registers a low image, especially among the youth of the society, businesses respond by providing extensive information to schools, often free or at nominal cost. Many of the materials provided are especially prepared for classroom use. Reactions to such efforts are generally mixed. In a recent issue of *Today's Education,* the NEA publication that goes to their 1.8 million members, two authors wrote about industry-produced materials. Sheila Harty, of the Center for Study of Responsive Law, stated:

What's wrong with that [provision of classroom materials]? Isn't it a public service?

What's wrong is that industry may be taking advantage of school children as a captive audience for market advertising. Even in the production of public service information, a tax-deductible expense, an industry can find opportunity to improve its image and to promote its brand name. At present industry appears to be conducting an advertising campaign to counter the disagreeable image corporations have accrued through inflation, unemployment, industrial pollution, tax evasion, and corporate bribery in recent years. . . .

Further study of industry-produced teaching materials may reveal reprehensible bias that encourages capricious consumption, partisan judgments, and disregard for public health.[10]

[10]Sheila Harty, "Who Produced These Teaching Materials?" *Today's Education,* Nov.–Dec. 1978, pp. 62–63.

In a companion article, William E. Hug, at Teachers College, Columbia University, presents a different position:

> I can support a very different series of observations [from those of Harty]. First, some educational materials produced by industry are among the best available. Many others are at least as good as those produced by publishing houses. Second, educational materials, including those produced by industry, play essential roles in instruction. The pervasiveness of educational materials requires the objective application of criteria and methods for selection and use without regard to the producer or sponsor. Third, schools, government, and corporate industry are collaborating now more than ever before to increase the positive contribution each makes to society and also to increase the credibility that each group desperately needs.[11]

We cannot explore this topic in detail. We can only point out here that the perception of the materials and of the reason for providing them does vary. It is possible that business could prepare their materials with more objectivity and thereby gain greater respect in the educational community.

It appears that the most common relationship between schools and companies is via the public information office. Colleges, for example, have often been disappointed when the only speaker that is available for a discussion on a topic such as the role of business in the society is a member of a public relations staff. Furthermore, too often the speaker who does participate uses a prepared script and knows little about the company. In some instances speeches are written for company executives by advertising agencies.

One might well ask the question: Does business realize the impression this creates when a speaker looks ignorant about his business and is reluctant to answer questions extemporaneously? The student president of a state organization of business students commented about one of his state's meetings:

> We were so happy to get a speaker from one of the largest American corporations. We thought we would learn a lot. Well, it turned out that we got a lecturer who just represents the company. He had a very

---

[11] William E. Hug, "Are they Appropriate? That's the Question," *Today's Education*, Nov.–Dec. 1978, p. 63.

old-fashioned speech in which he told us that when he was a boy, he knew he was going to work hard so that he could grow up and be dressed up every day. His speech was ridiculous. Our adviser said we would be more careful in selecting speakers in the future and he said that we wouldn't bother to seek speakers from American corporations. Business could improve what it provides to schools.

Both the schools and business might well reap rewards for such efforts.

There are, obviously, many other barriers to consider as we attempt to fully understand why economic education is not a standard component of the school curriculum.

Next Steps for Economic Education

What I have done is at best a partial analysis. What is needed next is a wise, thoughtful, reconsideration of what is taught and where it is taught. We believe this review will lead to a renewed commitment to economic education. In fact, in some states where goals are being reviewed, we see just that happening. In the proposed goals for the State of Pennsylvania, for example, we find:

CITIZENSHIP. Quality education should assure that every child learn the history of the nation, understand its systems of government and economics and acquire the values and attitudes necessary for responsible citizenship.
WORK. Quality education should help every student acquire the knowledge, skills and attitudes necessary to become a self-supporting member of society.[12]

In New Hampshire the State Department of Education has been working closely with the New Hampshire Business ad Industry Association to develop an economics program for grades 1 through 12. This program, which is to be implemented

---

[12]*Pennsylvania's Response to Public Concerns about Student Achievement*, Office of Basic Education, Pennsylvania Dept. of Education, 1978, p. 13.

shortly, will integrate economics education into the curriculum as part of other subjects rather than as a separate entity.[13]

There is now a Board of Education requirement in the Commonwealth of Virginia that a unit of instruction on the free enterprise system be taught as part of a required course in Virginia and U.S. Government.[14]

There are other states where similar goals are in the process of being implemented.

Robert V. Horton and Dennis J. Weidenaar, through the use of a Delphi-like survey procedure, attempted to determine the goals of economic education by questioning more than 200 economic educators, economists, social scientists, trainers of social studies teachers, businessmen, and others. They came up with what they called a "consensus" goal.

> The aim of economic education is to improve our understanding of the worlds in which we live. Without this understanding we are frequently confused and unable to identify, analyze and interpret successfully the economic aspects inherent in so much about us. The goal reflects our conviction that comprehension of the economic realities of one's world enhances self-confidence and self-esteem. Accordingly, both intellectual and emotional barriers are lowered for the making of rational individual decisions, in the light of one's values, in both personal and social matters. Economics also provides frameworks and tools for rational individual discrimination among social alternatives, in the light of one's values. Hopefully, "better" social decisions will result.[15]

That statement, an effort at consensus of more than 200 people, deserves careful reading and reflection. I would state our goal more simply:

> To understand the world in which they live and work, our youth need to know what economic phenomena are and how these phenomena are analyzed.

---

[13]From a letter from Neal D. Andrew, Jr., Deputy Commissioner of Education, State of New Hampshire, Dept. of Education, Feb. 15, 1979.

[14]From a letter from N. P. Bradner, Director, Division of Humanities and Secondary Administration, Commonwealth of Virginia, Dept. of Education, Feb. 13, 1979.

[15]Horton, Robert V., and Dennis J. Weidenaar, "Wherefore Economic Education?" *Journal of Economic Education*, Fall 1975, p. 42.

Our reason for seeking this understanding is simply to enrich both the observations of their world and their decisions as individuals and as members of a society that strives to remain a democracy.

V

Economic Education and Minorities
by Walter E. Williams

Economic education is on an uptrend in America, and I applaud it. Today economic news *is* news, and the mass media act accordingly. Thanks to the miracle of radio and television, for example, the latest changes in the Consumer Price Index or the unemployment rate reach millions of American households in only a few hours, if not minutes after the news is released from Washington. In a sense, we Americans are awash with economic data.

Yet the need for deeper public understanding and saner public policy in economic matters rarely seems to have been greater than today. Energy. Inflation. Poverty. Unemployment. Weak productivity. All these problems and more bespeak of little grasp of economic principles at the broadest *and* highest levels of our democratic life. This reflection of mine seems especially true for minorities and their leadership.

Hence my question to economic educators: Are your means—i.e. program content—really in accord with your laudable end? Or as Finley Peter Dunne's Mr. Dooley put it: "It ain't the things you know that land you in trouble but the things you know that ain't so."

Thus it is probably incorrect to assert that the problems we face in America are a result of economic ignorance per se. Indeed, if this were the case, I could be quite optimistic and predict that the solution is well within our grasp. Rather, I believe some economic concepts, especially those embodied in much public policy, are deficient. Further, I believe attenuation of the American moral philosophy expressed in the U.S. Constitution and its Bill of Rights is a more accurate characterization of the problem that we have in modern America.

For essentially the U.S. Constitution expresses a philosophy of a social order which holds that the individual is the *end*, not the *means* of the good society. Our political institutions have as their primary function the furtherance and enforcement of those laws that promote the dignity and individuality of the citizen. For this to be possible there must be political and economic freedom. While there exists the possibility for considerable debate on what precisely describes these freedoms, it is generally conceded that one of its necessary conditions is the absence of centralized economic and political power.

Thus in the economic sphere our Founding Fathers, as well as generations of Americans, promoted relatively free markets or what is called capitalism as a method of social organization most consistent with the dignity and individuality of the individual. Capitalism, then, can be defined as a system where responsible individuals are free to pursue their own interests; there is open access to the right of voluntary exchange; and there are privately held property rights to one's person, goods and services. Much of the original intent of the U.S. Constitution is directed toward this goal of free markets. While the U.S. Constitution is a protector of individual economic and political freedom, its value in this role has been subverted by both the courts and the legislature so as to stifle and make impossible those very goals that it was written to achieve. Herein lies the problem for modern Americans, majorities and minorities.

One of the most important domestic policy issues that confront us today is: How do we help the less fortunate to become independent, enterprising and upwardly mobile? No one knows the complete answer to this question. This is evidenced by the failure of much legislation, thousands of cases of civil litigation, and billions of tax dollars to produce a solution.

On the other hand, it is quite clear that we do not help less fortunate people by destroying their best alternatives. While this statement may seem trite and unnecessary, it is a position often ignored in policy debate and formulation. In other words, many people assume that just because a policy *intends* to help the disadvantaged, it will in fact produce its intended effect. Effective policy which increases opportunities for disadvantaged people does not spring naturally from the well of good intentions. In fact, good intentions alone often produce the opposite effects—a point, I believe, that ought to be made in any economic education program.

The Fair Labor Standards Act of 1938

Consider this. The Fair Labor Standards Act of 1938 provided a minimum wage of 25¢ per hour which has been periodically increased until a $2.90 hourly wage was achieved in January 1979.[1] Defenders of the minimum wage law claim that it protects low-wage workers from substandard wages and exploitation by long hours. It is also argued that by preventing low wages, the minimum wage law functions as an anti-poverty weapon.

Many of the moral issues that have surrounded the minimum wage debate such as "living wages," "worker exploitation" and the like are quite difficult to evaluate. Why? Primarily because with moral issues it is virtually impossible to formulate testable hypotheses. Also because there are no falsification standards on which there is any common consensus. In other words, by some standard or another we all probably think that we are working too hard and getting paid too little. However, with economic analysis, we can make some cause and effect statements about the minimum wage.

In practice, legislated wage minimums specify a legal hourly wage that is higher than that which would have occurred with free market forces. When evaluating the effectiveness of this policy, we must keep in mind two important limitations on the powers of Congress: (1) while it is clear that legislative bodies have the power to legislate wage increases, unfortunately they do not have the power to legislate corresponding increases in worker productivity; and (2) while Congress can legislate the wage at which a labor transaction may occur, it cannot require that the transaction actually be made.

To the extent that minimum wage raises the pay level to that which will exceed the productivity of some workers, employers will predictably make an adjustment in their use of labor. Ex-

---

[1] The minimum wage has since been raised to $3.35 an hour, in Jan. 1981—Ed.

perience shows such an adjustment will produce gains for some workers at the expense of others. Those workers who keep their jobs obviously gain. Those who lose their jobs, or are not hired in the first place, are made worse off by the minimum wage law. Therefore, the general effect of the minimum wage law is that of discrimination against low-skilled workers. It lowers the chances for employment for those workers whose hourly output is less than the legislated minimum. Furthermore, the minimum wage law denies such a worker opportunities to upgrade his skills through on-the-job training. Why? Because employers are reluctant to hire and train an employee who has an hourly output of $1.50 all the while paying him $2.90 plus the usual employee compensation costs.[2]

Briefly then this is the major impact of the minimum wage law: the workers who bear the heaviest burden are those who are the most marginal in terms of their skills. These are workers whom employers perceive as being less productive or most costly to hire. In the U.S. labor force there are at least two well-identified segments who share the marginal worker characteristic to a greater extent than do other segments. The first group consists of youth in general. They are low-skilled because of their age, immaturity, and lack of work experience. The second group are some minorities, particularly the youth of those minorities who as a result of past racial discrimination and other socioeconomic factors are disproportionately represented among low-skilled workers. These workers are not only made unemployable by the minimum wage law, but their opportunities to upgrade their skills through on-the-job training are severely limited.

It is not an accident that it is precisely these labor market participants who are also disproportionately represented among unemployment statistics. Modern youth unemployment statistics, even during relatively prosperous times, range from two to four times that of the general labor force (adults). *Black* youth unemployment ranges from three to seven times that of

---

[2]Actually, the minimum compensation that an employer must make is higher than the legislated minimum. He must pay social security, accident insurance, and health and vacation benefits.

the general labor force. Further, black youth unemployment nationally ranges from two to three times that of white youth unemployment. Additionally, the extent to which black youths participate in the labor market is less than half the participation rate of white youth.

The economic effects of minimum wage legislation have been analyzed in numerous econometric studies. The weight of academic research, as opposed to that performed by the U. S. Department of Labor, points to the conclusion that unemployment for some population groups is directly related to statutory wage minimums and that these unemployment effects are felt mostly by non-white youth.[3]

Most Americans are familiar with the current unemployment plight of black youth, but not many are aware of unemployment statistics for earlier periods. In 1948, for example, black youth unemployment was roughly the same as white youth unemployment. In fact, for that year blacks aged 16 and 17 had an unemployment rate *lower* than their white counterparts—9.4 percent unemployed compared to 10.2. Also in the same period (until the mid-sixties) blacks in *every* age group were either just as active in the labor market or *more* active in the labor market than their white counterparts. Now both of these pictures are reversed.

---

[3]See David K. Kaun, "Minimum Wages, Factor Substitution, and the Marginal Producer," *Quarterly Journal of Economics*, Aug. 1965, pp. 478–86; Yale Brozen, "The Effect of Statutory Minimum Wages on Teenage Unemployment," *Journal of Law and Economics*, April 1969, pp. 109–22; Marvin Kosters and Finis Welch, "The Effects of Minimum Wages on the Distribution of Changes in Aggregate Employment," *American Economic Review*, June 1972, pp. 323–32; William G. Bowen and T. Aldrich Finegan, *The Economics of Labor Force Participation*, Princeton, N.J.: Princeton Univ. Press, 1969; Edmund S. Phelps, *Inflationary Policy and Unemployment Theory*, New York: Norton, 1972; Arthur F. Burns, *The Management of Prosperity*, New York: Columbia Univ. Press, 1966; Thomas G. Moore, "The Effect of Minimum Wages on Teenage Unemployment Rates," *Journal of Political Economy*, July/Aug. 1971, pp. 897–902; James F. Ragan, Jr., "Minimum Wages and the Youth Labor Market," *The Review of Economics and Statistics*, May 1977, pp. 129–36; Martin Feldstein, "The Economics of the New Unemployment," *The Public Interest*, Fall 1973; Andrew Brimmer, *Minimum Wage Proposals, Labor Costs, and Employment Opportunities in the Nation's Capital*, Brimmer & Co., 1978. Dr. Brimmer demonstrates the adverse employment and business migration effects of the minimum wage law in the Washington, D.C. labor market.

Can increased racial discrimination explain this reversal? Probably not. Did blacks have more education in 1948 relative to whites? No. The answer lies elsewhere; namely, the minimum wage explains most of the reversal. As stated earlier, the minimum wage law discriminates against low-skilled workers, and black youth are among the least skilled among them. It therefore stands to reason that they will be the most adversely affected. Economic theory and historical evidence demonstrate that the possession of low skills does *not*, of itself, explain unemployment. The fuller explanation deserves treatment, I submit, in economic education programs at all levels.

Occupational and Business Licensure

But the minimum wage law is only one of many market entry restrictions that reduce economic opportunities for disadvantaged people. Occupational and business licensing (and/or regulation) is another barrier to economic opportunity.

Federal, state and local regulations governing entry and the conduct of certain businesses and occupations have many justifications and intentions. Among those are the desire to protect public safety and morals, provide for "orderly markets," eliminate unscrupulous sellers, and provide for a fair rate of return. Apart from these intentions are *effects* of business and occupational licensing that can be analyzed through economic principles.

Government control over entry to an occupation is typically done through licensure laws. People who practice the trade without state permission are subject to criminal prosecution which includes arrest, fines, and sometimes imprisonment. Usually licensure laws have various minimum criteria that must be met as a condition for entry. These may include: prior schooling; citizenship; written, oral or practical competency testing; attendance at "approved" schools or "approved" apprenticeship programs; prior occupational experience; minimum age requirements; local residency requirements; and so forth.

Licensing laws are, for the most part, administered by "experts," selected from among those already practicing the occupation or business.⁴ These "experts," sometimes called commissioners, change and modify licensure laws and have full police powers at their disposal to enforce compliance among practitioners.

The general effects of occupational licensure is that of raising entry costs to a particular trade. Higher entry costs have predictable effects that are borne out through empirical evidence. The major effect of occupational licensing is that of reducing the supply of practitioners and hence making the incomes of the incumbent practitioners higher than would otherwise be the case.

The effect of occupational licensure on minorities is that of reducing income opportunities and upward economic and social mobility. One important way that licensing does this is through increasing entry costs. Requirements that a person enroll in school and pass written examinations—to list just two requirements—will have a greater adverse impact on people who have low incomes and receive poor public school education. Minorities are disproportionately represented in the class of persons so characterized.

An example of one form of occupational licensure will make this argument more concrete. Stuart Dorsey studied the distributional effects of occupational licensing of cosmetologists (beauticians) in Missouri and Illinois.⁵ He found that in both samples the black failure rate was two to three times that which would be the case if the null hypothesis were confirmed, i.e., race and the failure rate are unrelated. In the Missouri sample only 3 percent of successful applicants were black, compared to blacks constituting 21 percent of failures. Similar results were obtained in the Illinois sample: 38 percent of failures were blacks while only 11 percent of successful applicants were black. Dorsey further reports that blacks averaged more than ten

---

⁴About three-fourths of all licensing boards are comprised solely of practitioners in the occupation that the boards control. See *Occupational Licensing and the Supply of Non-Professional Manpower Labor*, Manpower Monograph No. 11, Washington, D.C.: U.S. Department of Labor, 1969.
⁵Stuart Dorsey, *The Occupational Licensing Queue*, unpublished manuscript, Center of the Study of American Business, Washington Univ., St. Louis.

points lower than whites when the years of education and training are held constant.

Both Illinois and Missouri require that cosmetology applicants pass a performance test in addition to the written examination. On this test the score is based upon the applicant's performance on a person chosen by the applicant as a model. All applicants, at the time they take the performance examination, are unaware of their score on the written portion. Dorsey reports that the failure rate on the practical examination is low in both states for *all* applicants—less than 13 percent. But more remarkable than this finding is that the characteristics that are important in explaining written examination scores have *no* explanatory value for the score on the practical examination. In other words, on the practical examination *race has no statistical significance* as an explanatory variable.

Put straightforwardly, the written examination acts to exclude applicants, mainly by race, whose performance exams indicate are just as productive as others. Thus Dorsey concludes that the occupational licensing of cosmetologists: (1) screens out people on the basis of characteristics *unrelated* to job performance; and (2) causes an overinvestment in education and formal training because to the extent that the training does not improve productivity it is, he holds, individually and socially wasteful. In addition, he argues, licensing serves to reinforce handicaps already suffered by disadvantaged minorities. I concur, and I wonder if the growing number of economic educators in our country would agree.

Business Licensing and Regulation

Again, business licensing and regulation have an adverse impact on minorities: They make entry more costly and hence restrict entry. For example, the taxicab industry would offer an excellent business ownership opportunity for disadvantaged people were it not for the restrictions.

The taxicab business is one in which there are relatively low skill and capital requirements to become an owner-operator. It is also one where a lucrative income can be earned. However, some cities, most notably New York City, require that a would-be owner-operator purchase a license (medallion) in order to operate a taxicab. The current selling price for such a license in New York is $68,000! Chicago, Baltimore, Boston, Philadelphia and many other large cities require the payment of similar high fees as a condition for taxicab ownership. Clearly, the overwhelming effect of high license prices is to preclude the entry into the taxicab business by disadvantaged people.

In Washington, D. C., the taxicab story is quite different. Fee requirements for entry are nominal—less than $100. As a consequence, black taxicab ownership is high relative to the black population. Furthermore, the price of taxicab service in Washington is low relative to other major cities in the United States. Service received by patrons is better—Washington, D. C. has more taxicabs per capita than any other city in the U. S.[6]

Another potential business opportunity for minority entry is the trucking industry. It is another business opportunity where one does not need high levels of education and large amounts of capital. But because of government regulations, minority entry is seriously precluded. To own and operate a truck for the purposes of interstate shipment of goods requires that one receive an authorization certificate from the Interstate Commerce Commission (ICC). A certificate will be granted only if the applicant can prove that he can provide a service that no other trucking company is currently providing. For an applicant to apply for such authorization rights, he must retain a lawyer and bear expensive legal costs which, if borne, is still no guarantee that he will ultimately be authorized to operate a truck across state lines. If the applicant only offers to provide a better service at cheaper prices, he will surely be denied a certificate. Behind the ICC are the Teamsters Union and trucking companies who benefit from restricted entry in the form of higher wages and profits. Both parties exert considerable influence in the Congress to insure the continuance of their government-protected monopolized market.

---

[6]The District of Columbia has 7,700 taxis in operation compared to much larger cities such as Los Angeles (450), Detroit (2,300), Chicago (4,600), Boston (1,525), and Philadelphia (600). Only New York has a larger number, 11,300; still the number of taxis per capita is considerable less than that in the District.

At the state level of truck regulation, more interesting effects of regulation have been felt. When Daniel Walker won the election for governorship in Illinois in 1972, he had the political support of the Teamsters Union and the Trucking Association. The way he paid his political debt to them was to have his state troopers erect barricades around Illinois for the purpose of arresting truckers transporting goods without state authorization. The majority of those arrested on the first day of the crackdown were black truckers. From the national point of view, the fact that there are very few blacks licensed to be common carriers (although several have applied) points out the adverse racial effects of regulation in the trucking industry. There is not a single black trucker with the rights to move goods across all the forty-eight contiguous states.

The market entry restrictions cited here and market restrictions in general are not racial in the stated intent.[7] To the contrary, the stated intentions are those of high social ideals such as orderly markets, fair rates of return, consumer protection, and so on. Whatever the stated intentions of the regulations, the effects are racial to the extent that these market restrictions discriminate most against late-comers, poor people, and those without political clout. Minorities are disproportionately represented in such a group, and I ask economic educators to take note.

Denial of Human Rights

It is possible to find literally hundreds of examples of government-sanctioned market restrictions that have an adverse impact on the opportunity available to disadvantaged people. In all of these examples, we could demonstrate that raw racial discrimination does *not* adequately explain reduced opportunities for

[7]Note, however, that at the turn of the century white plumbers in the U.S. advocated licensing of plumbers as an effective way for preventing blacks from following the trade. See Sterling D. Spero and Abram L. Harris, *The Black Worker*, New York: Columbia Univ. Press, 1931, pp. 477ff. It is also interesting to note that during the 1930s most licensure laws were modified to require U.S. citizenship. This happened to coincide with the large migration of Jews to the United States as a result of the hostilities in Europe. I leave it up to the reader to decide whether these were unrelated events.

minorities. Instead reductions in personal liberty explains better the plight that many blacks face today. Discerning the causes of reductions in personal liberty in the United States cannot be achieved through a search for men of evil lurking in the halls of the federal bureaucracy.

A more productive search would be directed toward institutional and legal changes, promoted by men of good will, which have led to social outcomes that even they abhor. To avert ultimate tragedy, I believe that we, as a nation, will have to reevaluate our most cherished societal ambitions to see whether in the pursuit of these ambitions we endanger the survival of a system of social organization that has so far in the history of man produced "the greatest good for the greatest number."

A useful characterization of the problem that confronts us today is that there have been political changes that have significantly modified the free enterprise system. The free enterprise system rests on the right of individuals to own and control their own resources.[8] The free enterprise system, through the important linkage of ownership and control, minimizes the capacity of one person to coerce another. Furthermore, with extensive private ownership and control over productive resources the coercive powers of the state are minimized. The powers of the state are then restricted to the role of enforcing constitutional order and providing certain public goods such as national defense, public health, and highway construction.

As implied in my earlier discussion, the basic problem that disadvantaged minorities face is the enhanced role of government in the day-to-day activities of modern society, particularly government's role as a granter of privileges. Privilege-granting is the practice where the federal, state or local government confers rights and opportunities to some citizens and denies these same rights and opportunities to others.

The practice of granting government privilege is not a modern phenomenon. It has a history which dates back far beyond the Dark Ages where guilds and mercantile associations controlled

---

[8]High taxes constitutes a significant modification of ownership rights. Unnecessary government regulation also modifies control rights over resources. Both reduce private property rights over productive resources which include one's own labor resources.

trade in their particular area by association by-laws. Where guilds became rich and powerful they naturally wished to remain so and become even richer. This required that they continue to eliminate new rivals. They did this mainly by appealing for government assistance and obtaining charters from the king. This made the by-laws of the guilds and mercantile associations the law of the land which all had to obey.

Much of today's regulation and licensing differs neither in style or purpose from the medieval guild and mercantile restrictions. Virtually every major economic entity seeks favors and privileges from government. Note the presence of business and labor in the form of major headquarters close to Congress in Washington and the resources they spend influencing Congressional decisions. Almost every group in the nation has come to feel that government owes special privileges or favors to it.

—Manufacturers feel that the government owes them protective tariffs.
—Farmers feel that the government owes them crop subsidies.
—Coastal areas feel that the government should give them funds for rivers and harbors.
—Organized labor feels that the government should keep their jobs protected from competition with those who are not union members.
—Intellectuals feel that the government should give them funds for research.
—The unemployed and the unemployable feel that the government owes them a living.
—Big business feels that the government should protect them from the rigors of open market competition.
—Almost every occupation, profession or trade feels that the government, through licensing, should protect their incomes from competition that would be caused by others entering the trade.

I ask: Should not economic education programs take note of these things?

The first thing to be recognized about government privilege-granting is that government itself has no resources; it gets its resources from the people it governs. This means that when government grants one group a privilege, it must take a privilege from some other group of people, thereby handicaping this other group. Government must then grant the disadvantaged group a favor or privilege to offset their disadvantage. A particularly insightful view of the dilemma created by government privilege-granting was summarized in the Negro play, "Green Pastures," where God said to the angel Gabriel, "Every time Ah passes a miracle, Ah have to pass fo' or five mo' to ketch up with it."

Conclusion

The basic problem of blacks today is not, as I have alluded, one of racial discrimination per se; it is more a problem of government restraints on the operation of free markets which comes as a result of government granting various interest groups privileges and special favors.

Often overlooked in the attempt to find a solution to the problems of blacks and Hispanics is the fact that if there is a distinguishing characteristic of the United States, ours is a nation of minorities. Virtually all of its minorities faced persecution and hostilities and were despised; careful reading of ethnic history would point this out. But somehow these despised minorities were able to enter the mainstream of American society *en masse* without massive government expenditures and without "social commitment." The question now is, Why not today's disadvantaged minorities?

One of the most overlooked aspects of this question is that minorities in the past did not confront the barriers to entry that blacks and Hispanics now face. Take a poor, illiterate Italian in the 1920's, for example, who was industrious and sought upward mobility for his family. If he had the money to buy a used car, he could write the word "TAXI" on the car and he would be in business. Today more than a car and determination is needed. As stated earlier, to own and operate a taxi in New York requires the purchase of a $68,000 medallion. Needless to say, such a requirement seriously reduces economic opportunity.

There are numerous other examples of licensing and regulation that effectively restrict the entry and upward mobility of today's disadvantaged. States play an important role in erecting these barriers; so do labor organizations using the powers of the state. In many employment areas, particularly in the crafts, a requirement of employment is that one be a member of a union. Not only do unions racially discriminate in membership, but they have incentive to reduce the supply of labor available so that their members can demand higher wages.

Many Americans condemn racial quotas as a solution to the economic problems of minorities on the grounds that racial quotas violate democratic principles. But the matter of racial quotas is not so easily dismissed. The reason is that the economic game is not being played fairly. It is widely acknowledged by academic economists that public policy such as the minimum wage law, national labor law confering monopoly power on unions, and many other market interferences, discriminate against whole classes of people.

More specifically, we have laws which require union membership for some jobs. Given that some unions find ways to restrict minority membership, racial quotas may be a necessary second best solution if minorities are going to have employment opportunities in the trade. The "first best" solution, in keeping with democratic principles, would be to eliminate the government-conferred union monopoly. Mind you, I am not critical of the union idea as such, but only of government-conferred monopoly power. It would seem to me that those who find *racial group* membership an offensive criterion for employment should, for consistent application of those democratic principles, find *union group* membership an equally offensive criterion.

What are we to do in terms of ensuring equal opportunity to compete? The larger question is: What are we to do in terms of insuring wider *and* deeper economic education to help preclude the kinds of anti-minority and, indeed, anti-people legislation which I have detailed?

By all means, let us proceed with economic education but let the emphasis be on sound economic principles—principles that lend themselves to empirical testing. To revert back to Finley Peter Dunne's Mr. Dooley and his comment on education: "Children shudden't be sint to school to larn, but to larn how to larn."

Biographical Information

G. L. BACH
Frank E. Buck Professor of Economics and Public Policy Graduate School of Business Stanford University

G. L. Bach is Frank E. Buck Professor of Economics and Public Policy in the Graduate School of Business and the Department of Economics at Stanford University. He came to Stanford in 1966 from Carnegie Institute of Technology where he had served since 1946 as Dean of the Graduate School of Industrial Administration, among other posts.

Dr. Bach was born in Victor, Iowa, and received his A.B. from Grinnell College and his Ph.D. in economics from the University of Chicago. From 1941 to 1946, he served as Economist and Special Assistant to the Board of Governors of the Federal Reserve Board, and served briefly as Chief Economist in the United States Department of Commerce in 1946.

Dr. Bach is a special consultant to the Board of Governors of the Federal Reserve System and to the Secretary of the Treasury, and in 1948 was on leave as Survey Officer in charge of the study of the Federal Reserve system for the Hoover Commission.

W. LEE HANSEN
Professor of Economics
University of Wisconsin, Madison

After earning his A.B. and M.A. at the University of Wisconsin and his Ph.D. at The Johns Hopkins University, Dr. W. Lee Hansen taught at the University of California at Los Angeles.

He served as Senior Staff Economist for the President's Council of Economic Advisers during 1964–65, after which he returned to the University of Wisconsin where he is Professor of Economics and of Educational Policy Studies.

He has authored or co-authored more than 75 articles and books on economics and serves as Associate Editor of the *Comparative Education Review* and as a member of the Board of Editors of the *Journal of Human Resources*.

Dr. Hansen is a member of Phi Beta Kappa and has held an Economics Research Fellowship at the Brookings Institution, a Post-doctoral Fellowship in Economics at the University of Chicago and a Guggenheim Foundation Fellowship.

MARILYN KOURILSKY
Associate Professor of Education
The University of California at Los Angeles

As Associate Professor of Education and Director of the Center for Economic Education at the University of California at Los Angeles, Dr. Marilyn Kourilsky has helped pioneer innovative approaches to economic education. Her particular fields of interest are experience-based instruction, corporate education, teacher education, communication theory and entrepreneurial/career education.

Dr. Kourilsky earned her B.A., M.A. and Ph.D. degrees at UCLA where she was inducted into Phi Beta Kappa. She won the Harvey L. Eby Art of Teaching Award at UCLA in 1976.

She has authored or co-authored four books in the field of economic education. The latest is *Beyond Simulation: The Mini-Society Approach to Instruction in Economics and Other Social Sciences*.

MARY ELLEN OLIVERIO
Professor, Graduate School of Business
Pace University

The author of several textbooks in business subjects, Dr. Mary Ellen Oliverio earned her A.B. and B.S. degrees at Fairmont State College (West Virginia) and her M.A. and Ph.D. degrees at Columbia University.

She has taught at Marshall University, and from 1954 to 1973 she was on the faculty of Teachers College at Columbia University where she rose from Assistant Professor to Professor of Economic Education.

Dr. Oliverio has been active in the National Business Education Association, the Eastern Business Teachers Association and the National Association for Business Teacher Education. She has lectured at educational and business seminars in the U.S., Puerto Rico, Canada, Peru and Italy.

WILLIAM H. PETERSON
Holder of the Scott L. Probasco Jr.
Chair of Free Enterprise
and Director of the Center for Economic Education
at the University of Tennessee at Chattanooga

Dr. William H. Peterson holds B.S. and Ph.D. degrees in economics from New York University and an M.S. from Columbia University.

During his academic career, Dr. Peterson has served as Assistant Professor of Economics at the Polytechnic Institute at Brooklyn; Assistant to the Dean, Associate Professor and Professor of Economics in the Graduate School of Business Administration of New York University; John David Campbell Professor of American Business in the American Graduate School of International Management; and Burrows T. Lundy Professor of Philosophy of Business at Campbell University in North Carolina.

His experience in business and government include stints as Economist of the United States Steel Corporation and Senior Economic Advisor to the United States Department of Commerce. Dr. Peterson has served as a consultant for General Electric, General Motors, Republic of the Ivory Coast, Republic of South Vietnam, Time, Union Carbide, and Manufacturers-Hanover Trust, among others.

WALTER E. WILLIAMS
Professor of Economics
George Mason University

Dr. Walter E. Williams is Professor of Economics at George Mason University in Fairfax, Virginia, and was formerly Associate Professor of Economics at Temple University in Philadelphia, Pennsylvania.

One of America's outstanding black economists, he has been written up in TIME and has appeared on the national PBS television shows "The Advocates" and "Free to Choose." He earned his doctorate in economics from UCLA. He has served as senior fellow at the Urban Institute in Washington and the Hoover Institution at Stanford University.

Dr. Williams has won an Honor Award from the Freedoms Foundation at Valley Forge and a Dissertation Fellowship from the Ford Foundation. He has published widely in professional and academic journals. He has given frequent economic testimony before Congressional committees.

Index

Advertising Council, 23, 27
Antitrust, 12
Bach, G.L., 2, 3, 88 (biographical)
Boulding, Kenneth, 26
Business Roundtable, 23, 27
Businessmen, also business, Chap. 1; 2, 3, 11–16, 18–21, 30, 69, 70, 85
Center for Economic Education, 2, 7, 8, 21, 37, 65
Constitution, U.S., 74, 75
Consumer, 4, 12, 14, 32, 35, 38, 41, 43, 49, 83
Economic education, 1, 2, 5, 18, 31, 32, 46, 50, 54–57, 61–64, 66–69, 72, 74, 87
Economic (il)literacy, Chap. 2; 1, 3, 8, 22, 25, 38, 39, 48, 49
Employee economic education, 9, 10
Entrepreneur, 44, 45, 49
Free enterprise, 7, 16–18, 60, 64, 84
Friedman, Milton, 24
Galbraith, John Kenneth, 24
Hansen, W. Lee, 3, 4, 6, 17, 22, 88–89 (biographical)
Human rights, 83, 84
Inflation, 30–33, 42, 59
Joint Council on Economic Education, 1, 8, 9, 24, 26, 57
Junior Achievement, 47
Kourilsky, Marilyn, 4, 6, 52, 53, 89 (biographical)
Kristol, Irving, 19, 20
Licensing, 6, 79–83
Malabre, Jr., Alfred, 24
Mandate, state-required economics instruction, 7, 34
Master Curriculum Guide, 9, 24, 26
Methodology, Chap. 3; 4, 34
Miller, Burkett, 2, 6
Mini-Society, 4, 39–45
Minimum wage law, 5, 76–78
Minorities, Chap. 5

Morality, 65–67
Nader, Ralph, 14
National Assessment of Educational Progress, 27, 36
National Association of Manufacturers, 23
National Task Force on Economic Education, 25, 26, 57
Oliverio, Mary Ellen, 4, 5, 7, 89, 90 (biographical)
Opportunity costs ("trade-offs"), 25, 35, 45, 46
Parents, 5, 40, 47, 48, 65
Peterson, William H., 90 (biographical)
Profits, 3, 17, 20, 21, 30, 31, 43, 61
Regulation, governmental, 17, 84–86
Responsibility for economic education, Chap. 4
Scarcity, 4, 41, 43, 45
Silk, Leonard, 24
Smith, Adam, 15, 22, 24, 67
Surveys (opinion polls), 1, 3, 13–15, 28, 30–33
Teachers, 2, 3, 5, 8, 25, 39–43, 54, 58–60, 66
Television, 36–38, 50, 51
Weidenbaum, Murray, 16
Williams, Walter E., 5, 90–91 (biographical)

The University of Tennessee Press
Knoxville